How to
Do Good
& Avoid Evil

How to
Do Good
& Avoid Evil

A Global Ethic from the Sources of Judaism

Hans Küng
and
Rabbi Walter Homolka

Translated by Rev. Dr. John Bowden

Walking Together, Finding the Way ®
SKYLIGHT PATHS®
PUBLISHING
Woodstock, Vermont

How to Do Good and Avoid Evil:
A Global Ethic from the Sources of Judaism

2009 Hardcover Edition, First Printing

Library of Congress Cataloging-in-Publication Data
Küng, Hans, 1928–
    How to do good and avoid evil : a global ethic from the sources of Judaism / Hans
    Küng, Walter Homolka ; translated by John Bowden.
        p. cm.
    Includes bibliographical references.
    ISBN-13: 978-1-59473-255-3
    ISBN-10: 1-59473-255-8
    1. Good and evil—Religious aspects—Judaism. 2. Good and evil—Religious
aspects. 3. Jewish ethics. 4. Justice (Jewish theology) I. Homolka, Walter. II. Title.
    BJ1401.K86 2009
    296.3'6—dc22

                                                                                2009016181

10 9 8 7 6 5 4 3 2 1
Manufactured in the United States of America
Jacket design: Tim Holtz
Jacket illustration: © iStockphoto.com / iLexx

SkyLight Paths Publishing is creating a place where people of different spiritual traditions come together for challenge and inspiration, a place where we can help each other understand the mystery that lies at the heart of our existence.

SkyLight Paths sees both believers and seekers as a community that increasingly transcends traditional boundaries of religion and denomination—people wanting to learn from each other, *walking together, finding the way.*

SkyLight Paths, "Walking Together, Finding the Way" and colophon are trademarks of LongHill Partners, Inc., registered in the U.S. Patent and Trademark Office.

Walking Together, Finding the Way®
Published by SkyLight Paths Publishing
A Division of LongHill Partners, Inc.
Sunset Farm Offices, Route 4, P.O. Box 237
Woodstock, VT 05091
Tel: (802) 457-4000   Fax: (802) 457-4004
www.skylightpaths.com

This book is dedicated to the
Hebrew Union College–Jewish Institute of Religion
in great appreciation for the conferral of
a Doctor of Humane Letters honoris causa
upon Hans Küng (2000) and Walter Homolka (2009).

CONTENTS

ACKNOWLEDGMENTS

Special thanks to Dr. John Bowden, a real friend, and his colleague Margaret Lydamore, who have prepared this volume for the benefit of its English-speaking audience. John Bowden translated all the material not already available in English.

This book would not have been possible without the wonderful support of Dr. Ulrich Sander, the editor of the German original, which was published with Herder Publishers in Freiburg. Equally helpful and ever involved was Hartmut Bomhoff, whose advice and guidance are genuinely valuable. Another name cannot go unmentioned: at Abraham Geiger College, Tobias Barniske was untiringly involved in the process of selecting the anthology and preparing the book for publication both in the German and the English editions. The college librarian Susanne Marquardt gave much support and assistance.

At SkyLight Paths the book found marvelous support in Emily Wichland and her team. It was great fun to work with all of them, and we benefited from their professionalism. Special mention must be made of Tim Holtz for the outstanding cover design.

Finally, our thanks go to Stuart and Antoinette Matlins, gems in religious publishing. With SkyLight Paths and Jewish Lights they have created a singular environment over the years for religious publishing in general and Jewish authors in particular. Their enthusiasm and hands-on optimism have been experienced as a true breath of fresh air. For this we and many others will thank them forever.

Our deepest gratitude is expressed to another friend, Karl Hermann Blickle, who has been much involved in Jewish-Christian dialogue in the past decades and who generously offered to provide the necessary funding to make an English edition of this book possible.

Hans Küng
Rabbi Walter Homolka

INTRODUCTION

A globalized world also needs a global ethic. That is the conviction behind the Global Ethic Project that the theologian Hans Küng launched twenty years ago. Religion teaches that "human beings are created in the image of God and therefore unassailable in their dignity." "Freedom is always only that of the one who thinks otherwise," said the Communist Rosa Luxemburg. The parallelism is astonishing. The idea that human dignity is unassailable seems to be a common conviction. Yet every news bulletin gives the lie to it; there are daily reports of people being humiliated, tortured, exploited.

Hans Küng makes us aware that modern civilization is vulnerable, and globalization makes clear the differences in the world between poor and rich, between the various cultures and religions. The world of globalization and the Internet stands for apparently unlimited openness and unlimited possibilities. At the same time, the need is growing for orientation and trust. Without an ethical will, without moral force and energy, the problems of the twenty-first century cannot be tackled properly, let alone overcome.

Evidently, the Declaration of Human Rights does not settle things. We also need a Declaration of Human Responsibilities. It is here that the Global Ethic Project, which Hans Küng promotes with such tenacity, begins. He sensed that centering the world on Christianity does not get us any further. There is a need for a worldwide exchange between the religions, between worldviews in general.

We are only at the beginning of the discussion about tolerance, identity, globalization, and the consequences of the insight that in this world today we are all minorities. In such a situation we must be careful, attentive, and moderate. As a Christian theologian, Hans Küng, for half a century, has been one of the important international thinkers who feels bound by this insight. It is Hans Küng in particular who has come to know and think through both Islam and Judaism with more admiration and respect than many others, while remaining true to his own faith. He has expressed this for himself in these words: "By following Jesus Christ, human beings in the world today can truly humanly love, act, suffer, and die; in happiness and unhappiness, life and death, sustained by God and helpful to their fellow human beings." That is something like a declaration of love for his own religion ... over and beyond any authority. His certainty about his own tradition and its core reality makes Hans Küng boundlessly open to people of other faiths. As early as 1964 in Bombay he said that the truth of the Gospel and the truth of the world religions can be related dialectically. According to Küng, finding Christian identity does not exclude the formation of an ecumenical consensus. Thus for him, the practical consequences for Christians are understanding, solidarity, and commitment of the church as the minority to the members of the world religions as the majority of humankind. Here was the beginning of the idea of the global ethic.

In the 1970s the Global Ethic Project developed further. Hans Küng came to the conclusion that despite all the differences in faith, doctrine, and ritual that must not be underestimated, similarities—indeed, agreements—can be noted among the world religions. All human beings are confronted by the same great questions, the primal questions about where the world and human beings come from and where they are going, about coping with suffering and guilt, about the criteria for life and action, and about the meaning of life and death. All religions are at the same time a message and a way of salvation. All religions communicate in faith a view of life, an attitude to life, and a way of life, and despite all dogmatic differences, they communicate some common ethical criteria. For Küng, these observations became the leading question of the 1990s: What is this common basic ethic?

As early as 1988 Küng wrote: "The fact that they are bound together in ethics could become a unifying, peacemaking bond between the community of peoples; it could contribute to a freer, more just, more peaceful life together in a world which is becoming increasingly uninhabitable." From here Küng coined the term "global ethic," which complements the globalization of business and finance. It should not be understood in a binding Christian way, but in a new interreligious, intercultural sense. Believers of all religions and nonbelievers in all cultures should find what they have in common. Despite all the economic globalization and cultural standardization, the religions are not growing together into a unitary religion. Rather, it is realistic to say that the religions maintain exclusive claims to truth against one another. To use American political scientist Samuel Huntington's words, "A person can be half-French and half-Arab and simultaneously even a citizen of two countries. It is more difficult to be half-Catholic and half-Muslim." So the claims to the truth of each of the religions become a peaceful ethical challenge and a task for dialogue between the religions. How much the world would have been spared had the religions recognized earlier their responsibility for peace, love of neighbor, nonviolence, reconciliation, and forgiveness! Over long years of work, Küng and his team of scholars have investigated all the great religions, described them in extensive monographs, and discovered how richly the religious "variety of species" has developed. But however different their rites may be, and imaginative their doctrinal structures, at one point they all agree: human beings are of unassailable worth. From this is derived the "Golden Rule," which all religions know: "Treat your fellow human being as you would want to be treated yourself." This in turn leads to the four commandments set in stone: "You shall not kill, you shall not steal, you shall not lie, you shall not misuse sexuality." Thus, Küng's vision is close to that of Judaism. Hans Küng has summed it up in the four statements: "No peace among the nations without peace among the religions. No peace among the religions without dialogue between the religions. No dialogue between the religions without global ethical criteria. No survival of our globe without a global ethic, a world ethic." These are a few succinct principles. Here the term "global ethic" sums up the possible contribution of the religions to ethical standards for a world society. In 1993 they became the "Declaration toward a Global Ethic" of the Council of the Parliament of the World's Religions in Chicago, which we have documented at the end of this book.

Its basic statement rests on Küng's conviction: "Where they want to, the religions can bring *fundamental maxims of elementary humanity* to bear with a different authority and power of conviction from politicians, jurists, and philosophers." All the great religions call for fundamental ethical norms and maxims to guide actions, which are grounded in an Unconditional, an Absolute, and should therefore apply unconditionally for hundreds of millions of people—even if, of course, they are not always followed in practice.

After Küng's meeting with Benedict XVI on September 24, 2005, in Castelgandolfo, it was said that the Global Ethic Project brings to light "the moral values in which the great religions of the world converge, despite all their differences, and which through their convincing meaningfulness can also show themselves to be valid criteria for secular reason."[1] During his trip to the United States in April 2008, Benedict XVI emphasized this notion to representatives of other religions: "As we grow in understanding of one another, we see that we share an esteem for ethical values, discernable to human reason, which are revered by all peoples of goodwill. The world begs for a common witness to these values. I therefore invite all religious people to view dialogue not only as a means of enhancing mutual understanding, but also as a way of serving society at large."[2]

Now one can take the philosophical view that someone with insight cannot do other than act ethically. Küng doubts this. For him, it is religion that first makes the commandments an unconditional obligation. That, at any rate, is the way in which Christian theology sees it.

Ethical action is also of central importance in the Jewish religion. God grants human beings the facility to distinguish between good and evil and to recognize the ethical way. It is for precisely this reason that God has given men and women reason, so that they recognize moral action and an unconditional obligation. In this book, it should become clear that alongside "election" as God's first love and a people with a special obligation and dedication, Judaism is a religion that emphasises the share of all human beings in God's salvation. I value the Jewish view of "good" and "evil," our doctrine of human beings and their possibilities in the light of revelation and its relation to human reason, and the Jewish esteem for all non-Jews. From this basic theological attitude and our rejection of mission, Jews can continue a dialogue with other religions in a relaxed way: in the knowledge that God has called all human beings to cooperate in the healing of the world. With the Noachide commandments we also show how this could happen.

So we address Christian as well as Jewish readers. Christians will meet a Judaism that can also speak to them because it communicates valuable ethical insights and principles to them from a new perspective. Thus what was alien becomes something that appears familiar to them from their own tradition. Jewish readers should get an insight into the universal message of Judaism, beyond the particular rites and customs of their everyday religious life. It should become clear to them how much Judaism speaks to all humankind, as well as through the religions that have their origin in Judaism. Thus it shows them the actuality and relevance of Judaism and its teachings for all men and women.

The doctrinal structures of the individual religions are and remain highly different. But different as the approaches are, we are convinced that they meet in fundamental central ethical convictions. There are core statements in normative texts of all the great religions that support the same kind of ethic. In the present volume, Hans Küng and I have selected those from Judaism. They are arranged according to the six basic requirements of the 1993 Chicago "Declaration toward a Global Ethic" of the Parliament of the World's Religions. The texts impressively bear witness to the universal message of Judaism: just action as a guiding religious principle. They show the important contribution that Judaism can make in the wider context of a global humankind.

Many paths lead to human rights and to human dignity, which are unassailable. It is to the credit of Hans Küng that they become human obligations from the sources of the individual world religions. This volume investigates the "global ethic" that has grown out of that from the sources of Judaism as a modern form of the Noachide commandments—for believers and nonbelievers alike.

Rabbi Walter Homolka

JUDAISM AND A
GLOBAL ETHIC

Hans Küng

Jews, Christians, and Muslims all live in one world. Often they even live in one and the same country, in one and the same city, not only in Israel and in Jerusalem but also in New York and London, Paris, Amsterdam, and Berlin. Peace between the three religions, which all appeal to the one God of Abraham, is a presupposition for peace in a city, a country, the world. However, peace prevails only where people do not hate, insult, and fight against one another but talk and communicate with one another. Thus, dialogue among the religions is the presupposition for reconciliation, understanding, peace.

THE NEED FOR A COMMON CORE ETHIC

For centuries, reconciliation between the religions was impossible. The differences between the religions, the prejudices—indeed, the mistrust—were too deep. The religions deliberately lived in isolation from one another. But the global situation has changed decisively.

Global politics, the global economy, and the global financial system play an essential part in determining our own national and regional destinies. People everywhere are gradually beginning to realize that there are no longer any national or regional islands of stability. And despite the marked splintering of national and

7

regional interests, the world is already so strongly interwoven in political, economic, and financial terms that economists speak of a global society and sociologists of a global civilization (in the technological-economic-social sense): a global society and civilization as a cohesive field of interaction in which we are all involved, directly or indirectly.

But the rise of this global society and technological global civilization in no way—and this is important to me—means a unitary global culture (in the spiritual-artistic-formative sense) or even a global religion. Rather, global society and global civilization include a new diversity of cultures and religions. To hope for a single world religion is an illusion, and to fear it is an unjustified anxiety. The diversity of religions, confessions, and denominations, of religious sects, groups, and movements in today's world is still confusing. They are there side by side, linked together, and set over against one another in a way that is impossible to take in, and they cannot and should not be put under one common denominator.

Yet there are common features in the religions. All religions—confusingly different though they are—are messages of salvation, all of which answer similar basic human questions, the eternal questions of love and suffering, guilt and atonement, life and death. Where does the world and its order come from? Why are we born, and why must we die? What governs the destiny of the individual and humankind? What can be the basis of moral awareness and the presence of ethical norms? And in addition to interpreting the world, they all offer similar ways to salvation: ways from the distress, the suffering, and the guilt of existence; pointers to meaningful and responsible action in this life, to a lasting, abiding, eternal salvation; deliverance from all suffering, guilt, and death.

Beyond question, as a human phenomenon any religion is ambivalent, as ambivalent as law, art, or music, which have been and still are massively misused. From a sociological perspective, religions, too, are power systems concerned with stabilization and the extension of power. They have a high potential for conflict.

But they also have a potential for peace that is often overlooked. Certainly, religion can stir up, but it can also pacify. Religion can motivate, foment, and prolong wars, but it can also prevent them and shorten them. For their purely strategic, economic, and political aspects, even today the social, moral, and religious dimensions of crises in world politics cannot be left out of account.

Certainly, the religions of the world are in many ways at loggerheads with one another. In all the great world religions, systems of thought and faith have developed that in the end are incompatible. But my fundamental question is: Must the religions of the world necessarily stand in opposition and dispute with one another? After all, peace is at the top of their agendas. Their first task at this time must be the establishment of peace with one another, so that with all available means, including the media, they can accomplish the following:

- Clear up misunderstandings
- Come to terms with traumatic memories
- Break up stereotypical hostile images
- Work through conflicts of guilt socially and individually
- Demolish hatred and destructiveness
- Reflect on what they have in common

But do the adherents of the various religions know what they have in common, particularly in ethics, despite their great "dogmatic" differences? By no means.

NO FALSE FRONTS

First, to talk of understanding among the religions is not to call on believers to form a front against nonbelievers. The Roman campaign of re-Catholicization under Pope John Paul II (1920–2005), especially in eastern Europe, which was euphemistically termed "re-evangelization", led only to the old war graves being turned over again; we do not need another division of society and political parties into clerical and anticlerical (e.g., as in Poland). In contrast to this, the Global Ethic Project calls for an alliance of believers and nonbelievers for a new common basic ethic.

Secondly, with respect to a minimum ethic, a minimum of common values, binding criteria, and personal convictions, the religions beyond a doubt have a special function and responsibility. What unites all the great religions has been worked out in detail on the basis of the sources. Where they want to, the religions can bring fundamental maxims of elementary humanity to bear with a different authority and power of conviction from those of politicians, jurists, and philosophers. One of these fundamental maxims is the rule of humanity: "Every human being must be treated humanely!" Another one is what we call the "Golden Rule": "Do not do to another what you would not want to be done to you."

People must be made aware that all the great religions call for certain "nonnegotiable standards": basic ethical norms and maxims for guiding actions, which have an unconditional, absolute basis and therefore should also hold unconditionally for hundreds of millions of people, even if, of course, they cannot always be followed in specific instances. But ethics often goes against the facts. In fact, time and again people act unethically. However, it makes an important difference whether ethics is held to apply in principle or whether it is evaded, overplayed, repressed, or forgotten, and whether people are aware of the guilt that they incur.

Here, the Declaration toward a Global Ethic, which the Parliament of the World's Religions passed in Chicago on September 4, 1993, offers concrete examples. It is an unprecedented step, considering the more recent history of religion, that a gathering of people from all the world's religions succeeded in agreeing on a basic text that formulates shared ethical principles and irrevocable directives. All religions can and should work actively and commit themselves. The issues are therefore:

- Commitment to a culture of nonviolence and reverence for life: "You shall not kill—or torture, torment, or violate!" Or in positive terms: "Have respect for life!"

- Commitment to a culture of justice and a just economic order: "You shall not steal—or exploit, bribe, or corrupt!" Or in positive terms: "Deal honestly and fairly!"
- Commitment to a culture of tolerance and a life in truthfulness: "You shall not lie—or deceive, falsify, or manipulate!" Or in positive terms: "Speak and act truthfully!"
- And finally—and all religions have the greatest problems with this—commitment to a culture of equal rights and a partnership between men and women: "You shall not commit sexual immorality—or abuse, humiliate, or dishonor your partner!" Or in positive terms: "Respect and love one another!"

From these four directives it is already evident that the idea of a global ethic is essentially also influenced by Jewish sources, in this case by the "Ten Words" (Decalogue). We must now look at this more deeply.

WHAT DOES CHRISTIANITY OWE TO JUDAISM?

What does Christianity owe to Judaism? Almost everything, we might say. Indeed, Christianity grew out of Judaism and remains rooted in Judaism.

1. *The origin.* Jesus, to whom Christianity appeals as its Messiah, its Christ, was a Jew. Of course, he grew up in a Jewish family, in Galilean Nazareth. His name is a good Jewish one, in Hebrew "Yeshua," a late form of "Yehoshua," which means "*YHVH* is my help." (*YHVH* is the biblical name for God used by the ancient Hebrews.) The holy scriptures that he knew and read, the worship that he attended, the feasts that he celebrated, the prayers that he spoke, were all Jewish. And after a hidden childhood and youth he was active as a Jew among Jews: His message is addressed to the whole Jewish people. His disciples, men

and women, and all his followers came from the Jewish community. And the earliest community of those who, after Jesus's arrest and execution and initial dispersion, gathered in faith in him as the one raised by God, were Aramaic-speaking Jews who understood themselves to be a group within Judaism.

2. *That which is abidingly held in common.* Despite a history that is cruel and full of conflict, especially after the time of the Crusades, and that plumbed its catastrophic nadir in the Holocaust, a common heritage has been preserved down to the present day:

     A. Like Jews, Christians believe in the one God of Abraham, Isaac, and Jacob, whom men and women may trust as creator, preserver, and consummator of the world and history.

     B. Like Jews, Christians use many elements (psalms) and many basic features (prayers, readings) with religious content from Judaism in their worship.

     C. Like Jews, Christians accept the collection of holy scriptures (the Tanakh, Hebrew Bible, or "Old Testament") that are the source of their common faith and numerous common values and thought structures.

     D. Like Jews, Christians are committed to an ethic of justice and love of God and neighbor.

That brings us also to the problem of a common ethic, a global ethic, as it is posed to Jews and Christians. But let us also pose the question about common features the other way around.

WHAT DOES JUDAISM OWE TO CHRISTIANITY?

What does Judaism owe to Christianity? Almost nothing, some Jews would say, apart from humiliation and persecution. But the balance sheet is not quite so negative. Brief reference needs to be made to three historical developments.

1. *Universality of belief in God*. Judaism is indebted to Christianity for the fact that the message of a universal God established itself even in the most remote corner of the Roman empire. Already at the time of Jesus, the monotheism of Judaism also exercised a strong fascination on many non-Jews, and therefore the Jewish mission had some success in the Roman empire. In the Hellenistic period, from the second half of the second century BCE, the Jewish Diaspora had extended widely, and a rather active mission prepared the way for making Judaism a world religion. But after the fall of the Second Temple, Pharisaism increasingly established itself, and along with it, an anxious and zealous fixation on the letter of the Torah, or the Five Books of Moses. The greater freedom of the Greek-speaking Jews toward the law had some difficulty making headway, and the allegorical interpretation of scripture as practiced in Alexandria by the Jewish philosopher Philo (20 BCE–50 CE) was to have more effect on Christianity than on Judaism. Moreover, it is a fact that the extension of belief in the one God of Israel, the creator, preserver, and consummator of the world, throughout the Roman empire is due not to Judaism but to Christianity.

2. *The Jewish Enlightenment*. The rabbinic Judaism of the Middle Ages rejected any radical critical questioning of the Bible and its original message, as striven for by the back-to-the-Bible movement of the Karaites ("people of scripture"), which came into being in the eighth century in Persia and Babylonia; it also made any serious reform impossible. Only in the eighteenth century did a paradigm shift take place: The great Moses Mendelssohn (1729–1786), the first really modern Jew, took up the ideas of the European Enlightenment. A philosopher from the school of Gottfried Wilhelm Leibniz (1646–1716) and Christian Wolff (1679–1754), he advocated an undogmatic, rational faith combined with a loyal observance of traditional Jewish

obligations and rites. For him as a Jew, the German culture shaped by Christianity and idealism was more attractive than the secularist and in part atheist French Enlightenment. Thus, Moses Mendelssohn, who strictly rejected conversion to Christianity, was an essential help in leading Jews out of their medieval ghetto (which they had initially chosen freely) and into modern culture. Through word, action, and his whole person, he was the initiator and symbol of the *Haskalah*, the Jewish Enlightenment, which radiated from Berlin throughout central and northern Europe.

The great revolution began in Paris three years after Mendelssohn's death, and in the same year, 1789, its supporters passed the Declaration on the Rights of Man, which also included Jews. All Jews who took the oath as French citizens were later to be guaranteed citizenship unconditionally. Thus, in the nineteenth century, Jews were incorporated into bourgeois society. After the Jewish-Hellenistic and Jewish-Moorish interaction, this is the third interaction in world history between Jewish culture and an alien culture.

3. *The Jewish reform.* As a consequence of the Enlightenment, there was a great controversy in Judaism over religious reform. Whereas in Christianity the religious Reformation was the presupposition for the rational Enlightenment, now in Judaism the rational Enlightenment was the presupposition for the religious reform: modern universal education; academic training of rabbis as preachers, pastors, liturgists, and teachers; a reformed Jewish liturgy in the vernacular with modern music (including the organ); and a modernization of Jewish customs, including food regulations.

Reform Judaism took shape in the face of Orthodox Judaism hostile to reform on the one hand and secularized irreligious Judaism on the other. Under the spiritual leadership of Abraham Geiger (1810–1874), Judaism was now increasingly understood as a prophetic-ethical religion— a religion of justice, mercy, and unconditional love of humankind. The Jewish philosopher Hermann Cohen (1842–1918) left as his legacy the book *Religion of Reason Out of the Sources of Judaism* (1919). In its liturgy and education, Reform Judaism emphatically brings to bear the universal dimension of the covenant with God and human religion.

THE BIBLICAL ETHIC ALSO HAS A HISTORY

Of course, neither the importance of Judaism nor that of Christianity for the history of humankind should be seen exclusively. The biblical ethic, too, did not fall from heaven, but has a thousand-year-old history. It is worth noting that there is no people without religion, far less without an ethic, without quite specific values and standards. Already in the tribal cultures there are unwritten norms that are not spelled out in a codified way, a family, group, or tribal ethic, handed down in stories, parables, and comparisons, which—if it is recognized as "good"—universalizes itself:

- A sense of mutuality, justice, and generosity (for example, in reciprocal giving)
- A deep reverence for all life (e.g., in regulating conflicts, punishing violence, and dealing with nature)
- Particular rules for the coexistence of the sexes (e.g., the prohibition of incest and the rejection of libertinism)
- Great respect for the old (and, at the same time, care of children)

It is striking that particular elementary model standards seem to be the same all over the world. In the view of cultural anthropologists, unwritten ethical norms form the "rock" on which human society is built. This can be called an original ethic, which forms the core of a common ethic of humankind, a global ethic. This is not meant in the sense of a single "original religion" that could be found (but is not, in fact, found) in some tribe or people. On the contrary, such an original ethic can be found in all possible tribes and peoples. So a "global ethic" has its foundation not only (synchronically) in the common basic norms of the different religions and cultures today. It is also founded (diachronically) on the basic norms of tribal cultures that became established in a prehistoric period (before the beginning of written sources). Even if not every norm were the element of an ethic that was originally already given, a global ethic as lived out today is ultimately based on an original ethic given in biology and evolution and tested throughout time. But what does this mean for the ethos of the high religions—above all, for the Bible—that is common to Jews and Christians alike?

Only after periods of acclimatization and testing did a general recognition of such lived-out norms come about, norms that were later also formulated as propositions. Indeed, in some cultures, they have been put under the will of the one God. This happens in exemplary fashion in the Ten Commandments of the Hebrew Bible; according to the Sinai tradition, Israel received them after a divine revelation: not only "Do not murder, steal, bear false witness, or commit adultery," but also "I am the Lord your God ... you shall not ...!" (Exod. 20:1–14; Deut. 5:6–18).

Of course, the Ten Commandments, too, have undergone a history. This is true not only for the later ethic of the prophets and the still later ethic of the wisdom literature—which already sounds very "secular"—but also for the early ethic of the Mosaic law. At all events the directives of the "second tablet" for interpersonal relations go back into the pre-Israelite, seminomadic moral and legal traditions; they have countless analogies in the Near East. That does not exclude the possibility that a series of easily remembered basic directives were already brought from the wilderness by the group around Moses and inherited by all Israel.

But whatever the origin of the Ten Commandments may be, in their origin these fundamental minimal demands for a human life in community precede the Jewish belief in God and, if we compare them with the ethic of the peoples from Egypt to Mesopotamia, they are not specifically Israelite. What, then, is specifically Israelite? It is the fact that these demands are set under the authority of a covenant with God, to which the obligations of the "first tablet" and the fundamental commandment of the bond with *YHVH* alone, excluding all other deities, refer.

Thus, the peculiar character of biblical morality does not consist in finding new ethical norms but in the fact that the directives handed down have been put under the legitimating and protective authority of the one true God and God's covenant. The norms that came into being on the basis of human experience are not a voluntary human law for Israel or a general law of God, but the categorical, unconditional demands of the one true God who is known from history. Acceptance of the existing ethic into the new relationship with God produces a new motivation for morality: Gratitude, love, the gaining of life, and the gift of freedom become decisive motifs. At the same time, to make it more dynamic, existing norms are taken further, and new ones developed or taken over.

The Ten Commandments, also called the "Ten Words" or the Decalogue, are unalterable commands that express universal ethical and religious principles, a fundamental ethic that is set under the will of God. In the Greek Septuagint translation of the Hebrew Bible and the New Testament, "Torah" is narrowed down to *nomos*, in English translated as "law." Torah, however, does not originally mean a corpus of law but instruction generally—a pointer to a truly human life that is made possible and demanded by God.

Christianity has taken over these Ten Commandments word for word, and toward the end of the Meccan period—in the context of the vision of a nocturnal ride by the Prophet to Jerusalem—the Qur'an, too, offers a summary of the most important ethical obligations with a striking number of parallels (except for those relating to the Sabbath) to the Decalogue (Surah 17:22–38). So we can speak of a common basic ethic of the three prophetic religions.

A long process of development then made the original "instruction" an all-embracing corpus of law. If the covenant ethic at its center seems originally to be the announcement of the unconditional will of God, as irrefutable divine law, that does not mean that all legal materials in the Book of the Covenant cited in the Book of Exodus, and less so the whole wealth of further legal regulations—in part very detailed, with the character of civil or cultic law—go back to the event on the mountain of God.

BEING IN THE IMAGE OF GOD AND THE ETHIC OF HUMANKIND

"Adam" is very often understood simply as the proper name of the first human being. But "Adam" is synonymous with the Hebrew word for human being (*adam* = human being). The generic name has become a proper name because Genesis wanted to typify the whole genre in the first human being. In fact, the so-called Creation narratives in Genesis 2–4 are not folktales about the first human being in the Garden of Eden. They are about the definition of the situation of human beings generally, about the "Adam" who is the image of all human beings.

This also means that the first human being is not, say, a Jew (the history of Israel begins after the stories of Creation and the patriarchs). Nor is he a Christian (as a typological-allegorical Christian exegesis sometimes suggests), nor is he a Muslim (at least if one does not simplify and equate Muslim with monotheist). Rather, Adam is simply the human being (*adam*), and every human being is in God's image and likeness (Gen. 1:26–28).

From the beginning, the universal horizon of the Hebrew Bible shows itself here. It is about the one God, beside whom there is no other, and thus also about the human being, any human being, and not just about a single people but about humankind as a whole.

JUDAISM'S UNIVERSAL GIFT

An Ethic for Humankind

Walter Homolka

Hans Küng has already pointed out the tremendous importance of Abraham Geiger and Hermann Cohen for modern
Judaism. Both emphasized the dominance of the rational human
element in the Jewish tradition and the universal message of
Judaism that there is one God, beside whom there is no other, and
that there is the human being, any human being. Judaism is not
just about peoplehood but about humankind as a whole. As rec-
tor of the Abraham Geiger College, I feel indebted to the name
and work of Abraham Geiger (1810–1874), that great liberal
thinker in nineteenth-century Judaism. His work guides our
efforts to train rabbis in building a bridge between tradition and
modernity. One of Geiger's principles is particularly important for
our theme. It runs: "Through investigation of the particular to
knowledge of the universal, through acquaintance with the past to
understanding of the present time, through reason to faith."[1]

REASON LEADS TO FAITH

If reason leads us to faith, then this expectation expresses great
confidence in the capacity of human beings for rational knowledge. Abraham Geiger is not the only Jew to have this confidence.
Hermann Cohen (1842–1918), the founder of the neo-Kantian

Marburg School, developed the approach that reason is the underlying principle of revelation: "Reason does not begin with history, but history has to begin with reason. For the beginning has to be more than a temporal beginning; it has to mean the eternal originative principle."[2] Thus, Cohen sees the revelation event on Sinai as placed entirely in the human heart. Therefore, the title of Cohen's magnum opus of 1919 is programmatic: *Religion of Reason: Out of the Sources of Judaism*. In it and in his *Ethics of the Pure Will* it becomes clear that for Hermann Cohen Judaism is the best—though not the only—example of a religion of reason.[3]

HUMAN PARTNERSHIP IN REVELATION

Is this optimistic view of reason due only to Geiger and Cohen's idealistic-rational environment, or are we led into the depths of the understanding of the dialectic between revelation and reason in Judaism?

According to the Jewish view, in the revelation event on Sinai Moses received from God not merely the Torah in the sense of the Hebrew Bible (i.e., the "written Torah") but also the "oral Torah." This is the key that alone enables access to the complete understanding of the written Torah. As its name suggests, this "oral Torah" was handed down by word of mouth over many generations and finally found its written expression in the rabbinic literature. The twofold Torah contains the law revealed by God with its moral and ritual elements. The form of these laws is the product of an ongoing discourse, which produces decisions for new situations in other eras and thus makes change possible and continuity tangible.

Judaism as such has changed and altered at all times. It has harmonized the faith of the patriarchs with the legislation on Sinai, with the idealism of the prophets, with the practical concerns of the Rabbis. It has taken into account the social conditions of different eras and reacted to contemporary lifestyles and attitudes, though it has not imitated these compulsively.

It is possible to "believe" only in that which has previously been experienced as a commandment and heard as an answer to the questions of our own life. This relativization is evident above all in the Talmudic period, in which there was lively discussion and critical examination of the principles of Jewish law. Customs that could no longer be continued were successfully abolished by the special way in which the Rabbis read texts and by a process of interpretation that gave other meanings to the literal senses of the Torah.

Thus, so many conditions were attached to the death penalty customary in the biblical literature that it became impossible to impose it. In a similar way, the principle "an eye for an eye, a tooth for a tooth" (Exod. 21:24) was dissociated from any physical retribution and referred to financial compensation.

Later, rabbinic decisions were used to to do away with laws that had negative effects. For example, Hillel (20 BCE–20 CE) made it possible to enforce the repayments of credits even during the sabbatical year, not allowing them to lapse, as the Bible commands. Hillel permitted a declaration made in court, before the execution of a loan, to the effect that the law requiring the release of debts upon the entrance of the sabbatical year shall not apply to the loan to be transacted. This declaration was attested by witnesses or by the judges of the court before whom the declaration was made (*Mishnah Shevi'it* 10:4). As a further example of the degree to which traditional Judaism approved of changes in the past, it should be pointed out that in the second century CE the Sabbath services lasted an hour, the passage from the Torah was translated into the vernacular, prayers were different in each community, men did not cover their heads, they were allowed to have more than one wife, and men presumably sat with their wives during worship.[4]

So to sum up we can state that Judaism believes in a progressive process of revelation. It begins from the presupposition that the will of God discloses itself in an ongoing way and can be interpreted differently from the interpretations of the past. This concept of revelation makes it possible to relativize the written

Torah by the corrective of the oral Torah—that is through interpretative interventions—which in turn build the bridge between
rational insight and the text of the revelation. We can begin from
the fact that such questions were discussed by Talmudic scholars
in free ideological exchanges with representatives of the contemporary philosophies.[5] The various denominations within Judaism
differ in the intensity with which they accept this interpretative
intervention for modernity. But we can note this interpretative
flexibility in advance.

REASON AND REVELATION IN RABBINIC LITERATURE

This spiritual mobility must have its foundation in the relationship between scripture and tradition. That raises the question of
what view the rabbinic literature puts forward on the relationship
between reason and revelation.

In the Mishnah (the compilation of Jewish oral law), the
midrashim (the compilation of commentaries on the Tanakh), and
the two Talmuds (the compendiums of rabbinic discussions), different positions on the relationship between reason and revelation
emerge. Common to them is the fact that independent human
reason always accompanies revelation. There is the view that the
whole revelation was already given to Moses. This also already
contained the breadth of interpretations included in it. Thus we
read in *Pirke Avot* (*Sayings of the Fathers*):

> Ben Bag Bag used to say, Turn it [the Torah], and turn it, for
> everything is in it. Reflect on it and grow old and gray with
> it. Don't turn from it, for nothing is better than it.[6]

The statement that we find, say, in the story about Moses
when he visited the school of Rabbi Akiva (50–135 CE) is quite
different:

> Rav Judah said in the name of Rav: "When Moses ascended
> on high ... the Holy One, blessed be He, engaged in affixing

coronets to the letters." Said Moses: "Lord of the universe, who stays Thy hand?" He answered, "There will arise a man, at the end of many generations, Akiva b. Joseph by name, who will expound upon each tittle heaps and heaps of laws." "Lord of the universe," said Moses, "permit me to see him." He replied: "Turn thee round." Moses went and sat down behind eight rows [and listened to the discourses upon the law]. Not being able to follow their arguments he was ill at ease; but when they came to a certain subject and the disciples said to the master, "Whence do you know it?" and the latter replied, "It is a law given unto Moses at Sinai," he was comforted.[7]

Here we find the position that revelation on Sinai has established only a certain framework. This is developed and enriched, modified or relativized from generation to generation by the interpretations of scholars. Accordingly, human reason is given a major role in the knowledge of what God requires of us human beings.

While our first example attributes a central importance to the revelation event, the reaction of Moses to Rabbi Akiva in the second example shows that in the rabbinic literature human reason is thought to be equally important.

The most frequent position, however, lies somewhere between the two. The following narrative is a well-known example:

We learned elsewhere: If he cut it into separate tiles, placing sand between each tile: R. Eliezer declared it clean, and the Sages declared it unclean; and this was the oven of 'Aknai. Why [the oven of] 'Aknai?—Said Rav Judah in Samuel's name: [It means] that they encompassed it with arguments as a snake, and proved it unclean. It has been taught: On that day R. Eliezer brought forward every imaginable argument, but they did not accept them. Said he to them: "If the halakhah [Jewish religious law] agrees with me, let this carob-tree prove it!" Thereupon the carob-tree was torn a hundred cubits out of its place—others affirm, four hundred cubits. "No proof can be brought from a carob-tree," they retorted. Again he said to them: "If the halakhah agrees with me, let the stream of water prove it!" Whereupon the stream of water flowed backwards. "No proof can be brought from a stream of water," they rejoined. Again he urged: "If the halakhah agrees with me, let the walls of the schoolhouse prove it," whereupon the walls inclined to fall. But R. Joshua rebuked them, saying: "When scholars are engaged in a halakhic dispute, what right have ye to interfere?" Hence they did not fall, in honor of R. Joshua, nor did they resume the upright, in honor of R. Eliezer; and they are still standing thus inclined. Again he said to them: "If the halakhah agrees with me, let it be proved from heaven!" Whereupon a Heavenly Voice cried out: "Why do ye dispute with R. Eliezer, seeing that in all matters the halakhah agrees with him!" But R. Joshua arose and exclaimed: "It is not in heaven." What did he mean by this?—Said R. Jeremiah: That the Torah had already been given at Mount Sinai; we pay no attention to a Heavenly Voice, because Thou hast long since written in the Torah at Mount Sinai, *After the majority must one incline.*

   R. Nathan met Elijah and asked him: What did the Holy One, Blessed be He, do in that hour?—He laughed [with joy], he replied, saying, "My sons have defeated Me, My sons have defeated Me."[8]

Here Rabbi Eliezer attempts, completely without success, to convince his rabbinic colleagues of the correctness of his halakhic position. Because he does not succeed, he resorts to miracles to support the correctness of his interpretation. And finally he appeals to heaven to aid him and the truth as he sees it. But the other side points to the principle of majority decision and rejects any transcendent intervention in the development of the interpretation.

MANY PEOPLE HOLD PARTS OF THE TRUTH

So the right decision is made on earth, not in heaven. And the principle of the majority decision raises the question what concept of "truth" Judaism represents. This becomes very clear through the following Talmudic story:

> R. Abba stated in the name of Samuel: For three years there was a dispute between the house of Shammai and the house of Hillel, the former asserting, "The halakhah is in agreement with our views," and the latter contending, "The halakhah is in agreement with our views." Then a heavenly voice [bat kol] issued, announcing, "[The utterances of] both are the words of the living God, but the halakhah is in agreement with the rulings of the House of Hillel." Since, however, "both are the word of the living God," what was it that entitled the House of Hillel "to have the halakhah fixed in agreement with their rulings"? Because they were kindly and modest, they studied their own rulings and those of the House of Shammai, and were even so [humble] as to mention the actions of the House of Shammai before theirs.[9]

In his commentary on this story from the Babylonian Talmud, *Eruvin* 13b, Rabbi Yom Tov ben Avraham Asevilli from Seville (1250–1330), known as "Ritba," writes the following:

> The rabbis of France asked: "How can it be that both opinions are the word of the living God, since one says that a certain thing is prohibited and the other that it is permitted?" They answered that when Moses went up to the heavens to receive the Torah, he was shown forty-nine ways of prohibiting and forty-nine ways of permitting each thing. When Moses asked the Holy One about this, he was told that this is to be entrusted to the sages of Israel in every generation and the decision will be in their hands.[10]

In both texts it becomes very clear how important it is for the Rabbis to respect the position of the other in discussions and not make their own opinion absolute. It is this insight that permits us to understand that there can be more than just one truth that one individual or group upholds at one given time. The content of revelation has been handed down to the two houses—Hillel and Shammai—since the revelation event on Sinai. However, proper understanding of it requires rational interpersonal argument. None of the positions depicted here interprets the revelation event on Sinai in terms of verbal inspiration. All three put forward the view that the revelation must be interpreted, that one must dig in it, "turn it this way and that," "present heaps and heaps of doctrines above each title," that is, research and interpret it.

However, the standpoints described differ from one another in respect to the content of revelation. One sees the Sinai event as complete revelation of the Torah; the other regards it as revelation of certain general contents that need human reason for further development. At any rate, Judaism regards revelation as something that can be interpreted in different ways through human reason. The ongoing process of interpretation thus becomes a constant process of revelation, which is rooted in Sinai but also leads beyond it. Truths and views hitherto hidden are discovered, and innovations arise through which the interpreter becomes a cocreator.

Thus, Reform Judaism regards the Torah as divinely inspired, but not as immutable. Here, Judaism advances the position that the Torah is a testimony to a shaping experience. The religious message has been heard from generation to generation and each time it must be interpreted anew. Its holiness consists in what it attests, not the way in which it describes something.

The revelation on Sinai can be interpreted in different ways through human reason as a separate source of insight. Every human being should look at it as if he or she had been directly present at the liberation from Egypt. It is thus a possibility for, but also the duty of, every Jew to strive for an understanding of God's demands and transpose them into his or her own time. The Talmudic quotation from *Eruvin* 13b shows how important it is to deal constructively with positions that deviate from our own view, to heed and respect them. In Judaism, no doctrinal view and no generation have a monopoly on the understanding of the will of God. This approach calls for a high degree of readiness for dialogue and willingness to learn—to be concerned enough to understand the other side, and on this basis put forward our own view of things responsibly. That constitutes the character of the oral Torah and provides the basis for the value of a progressive revelation. Within Judaism, respect for the diversity of opinions is a consistent expression of this understanding of revelation.

ACTIONS SPEAK LOUDER THAN WORDS

A programmatic thinker of Judaism, Rabbi Leo Baeck (1873–1956), expressed very well what the goal of our life before God should be: justice. But this is attained through works and achievements, through fulfilling obligations and struggling over the commandments. For religion is not meant to give a good conscience but to put the conscience in a constant state of unrest and challenge. Only then is it truly religion. It must be able and resolved to offer resistance to any creaturely power when it is a matter of defending the Eternal. With an orientation on moral action, the question of the believed "truth" of Judaism recedes into the background. "The Jew is challenged to venture the leap of action, not so much the leap of thought."[11]

HOW TO DO GOOD AND AVOID EVIL

But what about the moral ambivalence of human nature, the struggle between good and evil? Do we always want to choose the good with our free will? Through the centuries Judaism was at least clear and consistent about that: the good in us is the consequence of our being made in the image of God. God, says the first chapter of Genesis, created Adam in God's image (1:27; cf. 5:1). And one of the greatest rabbis, Rabbi Akiva, observes: "Human beings are loved because they were made in God's image. That they were created in God's image was made known by a special love, as it is said, 'For God made human beings in the divine image.'"[12]

This doctrine is central to the Jewish understanding of human nature. It has never been given up and is regarded as a necessary and sufficient explanation of the good impulse (*yetzer tov*), the voice in us that makes us choose and do what is right.

The Jewish interpretation of the story of Adam and Eve in the Garden of Eden therefore differs from the Christian interpretation. Before the Fall, Adam and Eve had the absolute capacity to distinguish truth from lie. But after they had eaten of the tree of knowledge they saw that they were naked. Moses Maimonides (1138–1204), the great medieval philosopher of religion, remarked: "Beforehand they had seen that they were naked, but they had no intimation of its meaning. Eating of the tree of knowledge meant that from then on the human being continually had to help the good to victory in a constant conflict between truth and lie. The human being can be a morally responsible being only when the capacity for responsibility is part of his nature. The possibility for good and freedom of choice are necessary consequences of the human being in the image of God." Here it is meaningful to take a look at early Jewish literature—for example, Ben Sirakh: "He clothed them with strength like unto Himself, and made them according to His own image…. He created for them tongue, and eyes, and ears, and He gave them a heart to understand, with insight and understanding. He filled their heart, and taught them good and evil."[13]

So Ben Sirakh judges human beings without exception to be responsible for their actions. But if that is the case, then the counterpart to the "good impulse" requires even more explanation. In the simplest of terms, the answer of rabbinic Judaism is as follows: Just as God created the good impulse, so too did God create the evil impulse (*yetzer ha-ra*), so that human beings have the possibility of and responsibility for choosing between the two. The noun *yetzer* is derived from the verb *yatzar*, "form," and therefore means something like "a fundamental aspect of human nature" or "a fundamentally human disposition." Of course, this raises the question of how a good God can create an evil impulse,[14] and the answer is that at least to a large degree, despite its name, the evil impulse is not fundamentally evil.

One or two examples of this idea can also be found in the Jewish literature of the Roman-Hellenistic period—for example, when Ben Sirakh says: "The works of the Lord are all good, and supply every need in its season."[15] Or, "God created man from the beginning, and he placed him in the hand of his decision."[16]

In the Hebrew text of Ben Sirakh, the word for "decision" is *yetzer*; in Greek it is *diabole*, "calumniation," or *diabolos*, "the calumniator," which in Christianity is given the meaning "devil" and comes from the same word. But if all of God's works are good, the *yetzer ha-ra* cannot be evil in itself. For example, the Creation narrative reaches its climax in the creation of human beings. At this point, the text says, "And behold, it was very good" (Gen. 1:31). Here the pleonastic (i.e., logically superfluous) word "and" is understood as a reference to the fact that human beings were created with two impulses, one good and one evil, and the verdict "very good" refers to both. But the midrash continues, "Can then the evil desire be very good? That would be extraordinary!" And then it explains, "But for the evil desire, however, no man would build a house, take a wife, and beget children; and thus said Solomon: 'Again, I considered all labor and all excelling in work, that it is a man's rivalry with his neighbor' (Eccl. 4:4)."[17]

This illuminating text makes it clear that *yetzer ha-ra* is a blanket term for self-preservation, pleasure, power, possessions, reputation, and popularity. These impulses are not evil in themselves. On the contrary, they are good in the sense that they are biologically useful. But they are extremely powerful, and if they are not controlled by a lively conscience, they can quickly lead us to disregard justice and the needs of others and do harm to them. In this sense—because it so often drives us to do wrong—the *yetzer ha-ra* is evil. But it does not need to be. The psychical energy for which it stands can also be directed to good ends: "He commanded no man to sin, nor gave strength to men of lies."[18]

FOLLOWING THE GOOD IMPULSE NEEDS DISCIPLINE

It is possible for human beings to control the *yetzer ha-ra* in itself. But the starting point is not that this is simple. On the contrary, "Who is mighty?" asks Ben Soma in the Mishnah. He answers: "One who controls his [natural] urges [evil impulses]."[19] The problem is, to put it simply, how we cultivate and activate the good impulse, so that we can exercise the necessary control.

The rabbinic answer is: through study, prayer, and observing the commandments.[20] To occupy ourselves with the Torah has a twofold significance in rabbinic Judaism. It means studying its teachings, for doing this means to be in contact with the thought of God and is therefore both a spiritual and an intellectual occupation. But to concern ourselves with the Torah likewise means to practice the way of life that the Torah prescribes—a way that both entails an ethical code and calls for religious discipline.

AN ETHICAL CODE FOR HUMANKIND
FROM THE HEBREW BIBLE

Because of the manifest importance and future bearing of the covenant with Abraham (which is confirmed through Isaac and Jacob) and then the Sinai covenant, that first covenant of all, which according to the Hebrew Bible God made with Noah, is often overlooked. With whom precisely was it made? With humankind as a whole, indeed with the whole of creation, with human beings and animals. After the Flood, God declares to Noah and his sons as the representatives of humankind that are left: "Behold, I establish My covenant with you and your descendants after you, and with every living creature that is with you, the birds, the cattle, and every beast of the earth with you, as many as came out of the ark. I establish My covenant with you, that never again shall all flesh be cut off by the waters of a flood, and never again shall there be a flood to destroy the earth" (Gen. 9:9–11).

This first covenant of God with human beings is not a bilateral undertaking—how could it be otherwise after the almost complete destruction of humankind?—and some exegetes think, contrary to the text, that it is illegitimate to talk of a "covenant" in the strict sense. Rather, it is a promise and assurance given by God, God's commitment and concern, but one that constitutes a covenant (in an analogous but real sense), a covenant forever with the whole of creation, God's covenant, which God "guarantees" and "establishes": the creation is never again to perish, and humankind and the animals are to be preserved.

So this amazing promise applies not only to the Jewish people but to the whole of humankind, uncircumcised and circumcised. It is a covenant with humankind, with no distinction of races, classes, castes, or religions. For the sign of this covenant is not circumcision, performed by the members of the chosen people. The marvelous symbol of this covenant with humankind set up by God is the rainbow, arching over the earth, which bears witness to God's reign, trustworthiness, and peace, towering over all.

However, it must not be overlooked that this covenant is already matched by a clear obligation on the human side, and to this degree it is two-sided after all. Before the promise of the covenant, some elementary demands are put to the new humankind that—unlike the later Torah—are to be binding for Israelites and non-Israelites alike. Granted, here we do not have specific laws for a particular people, but basic demands for the whole of humankind to ensure its preservation. The covenant with humankind is matched by an ethic of humankind.

THERE ARE "RIGHTEOUS OF THE PEOPLES"

With Noah and the commandments attributed to him, the rich written and oral tradition of Judaism provides rules of conduct that it can introduce into a discussion about the foundations of a common human ethic. Over the centuries of its development, Judaism has provided a legitimate alternative beside the election of Israel and its decision for the Torah of God: the righteous of the peoples. The other is not robbed of his or her identity, but becomes righteous through the rational knowledge of a universal fundamental morality that binds together all men and women and lets the stranger become a neighbor.

For both Jews and non-Jews, the notion that all human beings are in the image of God, which is essential to the Jewish religion, means that a way of knowledge to God stands open and all have the possibility of applying reason as a means to ethical fulfillment, to attaining freedom. The Greek Jewish philosopher Philo of Alexandria gives us an answer from an early Jewish perspective:

> No two things are so closely akin as independence of action and freedom, because the bad man has a multitude of encumbrances, such as love of money or reputation and pleasure, while the good man has none at all. He stands defiant and triumphant over love, fear, cowardice, grief and all that sort, as the victor over the fallen in the wrestling bout. For he has learned to set at nought the injunctions laid upon him by those most lawless rulers of the soul, inspired as he is by his ardent yearning for the freedom whose peculiar heritage it is that it obeys no orders and works no will but its own.[21]

But this possibility also entails responsibility for striving for the good. According to the biblical view, any human being can attain philosophical and theological knowledge by a discursive way independent of a specific understanding of revelation. For the human being has been created in the image of God and therefore has a share in divine reason. And anyone who behaves ethically has a share in the world to come.[22] Jews by no means believe that they possess the revelation that alone brings salvation.[23]

Rabbi Kaufmann Kohler (1843–1926) stated in 1910:

> Judaism, which is neither a mere system of religion nor a mere system of a people, but sets out to be a covenant with God which unites peoples, has no self-contained truth and does not address a self-contained part of humankind.... Christianity and Islam form part of the history of Judaism. Now between these world religions with their great cultural spheres stands little Judaism as a cosmopolitan factor and points to that ideal future of a humankind truly united in God which only in a ceaseless forward striving and in accordance with ever more perfect images of the promised triumph of the good, true and divine on earth, longs for the realization of the kingdom of God.[24]

It is fundamental to the trialogue among Jews, Christians, and Muslims that in the context of this Noachide covenant Jews can recognize Christians and Muslims as "god-fearers" (as is done by Kaufmann Kohler and some rabbinic authorities, in contrast to the rigorist Maimonides, who designates Christians as idolaters because of the doctrine of the Trinity and veneration of images), for they, too, have turned away from pagan deities to the true God. Therefore, even if alleged errors (e.g., belief in the Trinity) are mixed in with their faith, they can be saved, like the pagan Noachides, who were bound not to the commandments of Moses but to the Noachide prohibitions. In modern Judaism, for the same reason Christians are not regarded as pagans but as "children of Noah."

The stranger, who in Judaism is regarded as a "son of Noah," is here as much a creature of God as Jews themselves, concludes Hermann Cohen.[25] Through the seven Noachide commandments as a universal possibility of attaining righteousness before God, the theological concept of the human being as a creature of God becomes the political concept of the fellow human being, the fellow citizen.[26] Here the idea of the "righteous of the peoples of the world" comes into an interesting tension with the Jewish concept of election.

THE NOACHIDE COMMANDMENTS MAKE CONVERSION SUPERFLUOUS

The election of Israel can thus be recognized for what it is. Selection for a particular task and function in relationship with God by no means indicates that other human beings do not live equally pious lives before God and cannot attain righteousness before God. This becomes clear in a controversy between Rabbi Eliezer ben Hyrcanus (first and second centuries CE) and Rabbi Joshua ben Hananiah (died 131 CE) over whether the righteous of the peoples would have a share in the world to come.

For Rabbi Eliezer, only those born as Jews or those who have gone over to Judaism completely have a share in the world to come, because they are subject to the Jewish law in its totality.[27] By contrast, Rabbi Joshua puts forward the view that all of the righteous, whether Jewish or non-Jewish, have a share in the world to come.[28] In 1180 in the *Mishneh Torah*, the most important medieval codification of the Jewish religion, Moses Maimonides follows the view of Rabbi Joshua. He thus supports this view of justice.[29] The interpretation of the Noachide commandments as regulations purely of natural law and commandments of reason is not undisputed in the rabbinic tradition. According to Maimonides, their observance should not be subject to merely natural motivation but should also be an expression of the obedience of non-Jewish humankind to the God of Israel.[30]

A radical opinion begins from the fact that the Noachide commandments define only a minimum and that converting to Judaism is also required to participate fully in God's covenant. Thus, Izates, king of Adiabene in the middle of the first century CE, is advised by a Jew that it is enough if he remains a "god-fearer" (*ger toshav*), whereas another advises him to convert.[31] Yet other opinions were more pessimistic about the Noachides. However, such differences of opinion should not disguise the fact that converting to Judaism was an illusory alternative over long periods of history.[32]

Rabbinic Judaism does not require non-Jews who want to live in a community and in the same territory with Jews to convert to Judaism, to believe in the God of Israel, and to subject themselves to the traditional 613 prohibitions and commandments of the Torah. It merely requires them to observe the seven commandments that are traditionally associated with the covenant of God with Noah in the Flood narrative.[33] The other (*acher*) becomes the brother (*ach*) through the responsibility (*achrayut*) with which he acts in the commonwealth. And for Maimonides it is even possible to know the Noachide law with the help of rational contemplation (*hecre ha-da'at*—*inclinatio rationalis*).

JUDAISM REJECTS MISSIONIZING

Moses Mendelssohn also refers to the Noachide commandments, when he is invited by the Zurich preacher Johann Caspar Lavater (1741–1801) in 1769 to a religious disputation aimed at converting Mendelssohn to Calvin's Christianity.

In December 1769 Moses Mendelssohn counters with a reference to the tolerant attitude of Judaism, which rejects any missionizing:

> In accordance with the principle of my religion I should not seek to convert anyone who is not born according to our law. This spirit of conversion, the origin of which some are so keen to burden the Jewish religion with, is diametrically opposed to this. All our rabbis teach unanimously that the written and oral laws in which our revealed religion consists are binding only on our nation. Moses commanded the law for us, it is a legacy of the community of Jacob. All the other peoples of the earth, we believe, have been instructed by God to observe the law of nature and the religion of the patriarchs [Mendelssohn notes: "The seven main commandments of the Noachides"]. Those who direct their way of life in accordance with this religion of nature and reason are

called by other nations virtuous men, and these are children
of the eternal blessedness.[34]

With this statement about the recognition of other convictions by
Judaism, Mendelssohn rejects Lavater's demand for conversion. He
identifies the Noachide commandments with natural law. And as
natural law they are open to Lavater's rational insight.

So we may summarize: According to Jewish tradition the
Noachide rules give fundamental instructions for action by all
human beings in respect to God (the prohibition of idolatry and
blasphemy), fellow human beings (prohibition of murder, theft,
and sexual promiscuity), nature (prohibition against torturing animals), and society (commandment for a just society with just
laws). The Jewish sources from the Talmud through Maimonides
to Moses Mendelssohn and Hermann Cohen indicate that every
non-Jew who observes these commandments and prohibitions is
to be regarded as righteous among the peoples. Thus, non-Jews
attain the same spiritual and moral level as the high priest in the
Temple.[35] We have seen that the Jewish tradition designates such
a person *ger toshav*, a righteous non-Jew, and as "righteous among
the peoples" and accepts this person as such.

The dispute between Mendelssohn and Lavater has shown
that the Noachide commandments also constitute the starting point
from which Judaism enters into dialogue with all men and women.

A NEW RELATIONSHIP BETWEEN
CHRISTIANS AND JEWS

In recent decades good relations with the Christian churches have
developed. Judaism and Islam are likewise bound together in
diverse ways and stand in a brotherly relationship. However, the
open dialogue between Judaism and Christianity that is being cultivated today is the result of a long and painful process. First, the
link between "throne and altar" so predominant in European history had to be dissolved and equal rights for all religions had to be

established. Finally, the trauma of the Holocaust brought about a profound change within the churches about how to relate to Judaism. After World War II, churches had to recognize that Christian ethics and church leadership had failed miserably during the Third Reich when confronted with the task of effectively protecting their Jewish brothers and sisters from being murdered. This led step by step to the beginning of a new relationship between Christians and Jews.

I am firmly convinced that we must cultivate this relationship with everyone. The vision of a universal bond is endorsed by the Rabbis in *Midrash Tanchuma*: "At Sukkot the Israelites sacrificed seventy oxen for the seventy nations of the earth." Thus all were taken into consideration and remembered in the sacrificial cult of Israel.

According to Jewish teachings, the salvation of all peoples is grounded in the Noachide commandments. Thus, the Jewish tradition has always been very open toward the pluralism and the recognition of others. Hans Küng's Global Ethic Project argues along the same lines. It points to the possibility for all men and women to receive a share in the world to come and approval before God's face.

THE NOACHIDE COMMANDMENTS TODAY

In the rabbinic tradition the number of the elements of such a universal fundamental morality fluctuates between one and thirty.[36] But very soon the corresponding notion developed that the number of these commandments was seven.[37] Six of the seven commandments had already been given to Adam:[38] the prohibition of idolatry, blasphemy, murder, adultery, and robbery, and the commandment to establish courts of justice. The seventh given to Noah further emphasizes their universal character: the prohibition of eating a limb from a living animal, as it is said: "Only flesh with the life thereof, which is the blood thereof shall ye not eat" (Gen. 9:4). Thus we have seven commandments, concludes Moses Maimonides in his *Mishneh Torah*.[39]

In the situation of a non-Jewish majority society, increased importance was attributed to the grounding of the Noachide commandments in natural law. When John Selden (1584–1654), the English politician, jurist, and orientalist, published a book in 1640 about the Hebrew understanding of natural and international law, he put on the title page in Hebrew letters the Hebrew expression for the Noachide commandments. And Hermann Cohen explains: "As a Noachide he [the 'stranger'] is not bound to the law of Moses, but only to the seven precepts, 'the seven commandments of the sons of Noah…. And these seven precepts have a strictly moral character…. The belief in the Jewish God is not required."[40]

The Global Ethic Project of Hans Küng may be seen as a renewed, contemporary attempt to formulate the Noachide commandments in a way that is acceptable within a wide range of cultures and societies. In the beginning of the 1990s, Hans Küng was among those who proposed to pass a "Declaration toward a Global Ethic," which was prepared during a two-year consultation process with about two hundred scholars who represented many world religions. It was presented at the 1993 Parliament of the World's Religions, held in Chicago on September 4, 1993. The declaration, with "The Principles of a Global Ethic" appended, was signed by 143 respected leaders from all of the world's major faiths, including Baha'i, Brahmanism, Brahma Kumaris, Buddhism, Christianity, Hinduism, Indigenous, Interfaith, Islam, Jainism, Judaism, Native American, Neo-Pagan, Sikhism, Taoism, Theosophist, Unitarian Universalist, and Zoroastrian.

In the following six sections of this book, we use the six major principles of the Global Ethic Project as a structure to present the immense richness of the Jewish tradition:

1. **The value of the human:** *Every human being must be treated humanely.*
2. **The Golden Rule:** *Do not do to another what you would not want to be done to you.*

3. **Peace:** *Commitment to a culture of nonviolence and reverence for all life.*
4. **Justice:** *Commitment to a culture of justice and a just economic order.*
5. **Truth and tolerance:** *Commitment to a culture of tolerance and a life in truthfulness.*
6. **Equal rights:** *Commitment to a culture of equal rights and a partnership between men and women.*

For each principle we chose a key text of a major Jewish thinker explaining a central Jewish concept relating to it. After this follows a section of primary sources in chronological order ranging from the Hebrew bible to post-Enlightenment Jewish thought. Each of these study sections is headed by an introductory quote that aims to summarize the Jewish position.

What arises is an impressive argument that Judaism to this day is able to provide an ethical path of universal appeal. The Noachide covenant for all humankind and its commandments are guidance for everyone alive today.

Core Ethic 1

The value of the human: every human being must be treated humanely.

Sacred Image of Man

Abraham J. Heschel

The biblical account of creation is couched in the language of allusion. Nothing is said about the intention or the plan that preceded the creation of heaven and earth. The Bible does not begin: And God said: Let us create heaven and earth. All we hear is an allusion to God's creative act, and not a word about intention or meaning. The same applies to the creation of all other beings. We only hear what He does, not what He thinks. "And God said: Let there be." The creation of man, however, is preceded by a forecast: "And God said: Let us make man in our image, after our likeness." The act of man's creation is preceded by an utterance of His intention, God's knowledge of man is to precede man's coming into being. God knows him before He creates him. Man's being is rooted in his being known about. It is the creation of man that opens a glimpse into the thought of God, into the meaning beyond the mystery.

"And God said: I will make man in My image (*tselem*), after My likeness (*demuth*).... And God created man in His image, in the image of God He created him" (Gen. 1:26f).

These words, which are repeated in the opening words of the fifth chapter of Genesis—*This book is the story of man*. When God created man, He made him in the likeness (*demuth*) of God—contain, according to Jewish tradition, the fundamental statement about the nature and meaning of man.

In many religions, man is regarded as an image of a god. Yet the meaning of such regard depends on the meaning of the god whom man resembles. If the god is regarded as a man magnified, if the gods are conceived of in the image of man, then such regard tells us little about the nature and destiny of man. Where God is one among many gods, where the word "divine" is used as mere hyperbolic expression, where the difference between God and man is but a difference in degree, then an expression such as the divine image of man is equal in meaning to the idea of the supreme in man. It is only in the light of what the biblical man thinks of God, namely a Being who created heaven and earth, the God of absolute justice and compassion, the master of nature and history who transcends nature and history, that the idea of man having been created in the image of God refers to the supreme mystery of man, of his nature and existence.

Image and likeness of God. What these momentous words are trying to convey has never ceased to baffle the reader of the Bible. In the Bible, *tselem*, the word for image, is nearly always used in a derogatory sense, denoting idolatrous images. The same applies to *demuth*, the word for likeness.

"To whom will ye liken Me, and make Me equal, and compare Me, that we may be alike?" (Isa. 46:5). "For who in the skies can be compared unto the Lord, who among the sons of might can be likened unto the Lord?" (Ps. 89:7).

God is divine, and man is human. This contrast underlies all biblical thinking. God is never human, and man is never divine, "for I am God and not man" (Hos. 11:9). "God is not man to be capricious, or mortal to change His mind" (Num. 23:19).

Thus, the likeness of God means the likeness of Him who is unlike man. The likeness of God means the likeness of Him, compared with whom all else is like nothing.

Indeed the words "image and likeness of God" conceal more than they reveal. They signify something which we can neither comprehend nor verify. For what is our image? What is our likeness? Is there anything about man that may be compared with

God? Our eyes do not see it; our minds cannot grasp it. Taken literally, these words are absurd, if not blasphemous. And still they hold the most important truth about the meaning of man.

Obscure as the meaning of these terms is, they undoubtedly denote something *unearthly*, something that belongs to the sphere of God. *Demuth* and *tselem* are of a *higher sort of being* than the things created in the six days. This, it seems, is what the verse intends to convey: Man partakes of an unearthly divine sort of being.

An idea is relevant if it serves as an answer to a question. To understand the relevance of "the divine image and likeness," we must try to ascertain the question which it comes to answer.

Paradoxically, the problem of man arises more frequently as the problem of death than as the problem of life. It is an important fact, however, that in contrast with Babylonia and particularly Egypt, where the preoccupation with death was the central issue of religious thinking, the Bible hardly deals with death as a problem. Its central concern is not, as in the Gilgamesh Epic, how to escape death, but rather how to sanctify life. And the divine image and likeness does not serve man to attain immortality but to attain sanctity.

Man is man not because of what he has in common with the earth, but *because of what he has in common with God*. The Greek thinkers sought to understand man as *a part of the universe*: the prophets sought to understand man as *a partner of God*.

It is a concern and a task that man has in common with God.

The intention is not to identify "the image and likeness" with a particular quality or attribute of man, such as reason, speech, power, or skill. It does not refer to something which in later systems was called "the best in man," "the divine spark," "the eternal spirit," or "the immortal element" in man. It is the whole man and every man who was made in the image and likeness of God. It is both body and soul, sage and fool, saint and sinner, man in his joy and in his grief, in his righteousness and wickedness. The image is not in man; it is man.

46   HOW TO DO GOOD AND AVOID EVIL

The basic dignity of man is not made up of his achievements, virtues, or special talents. It is inherent in his very being. The commandment "Love your neighbor as yourself" (Lev. 19:18) calls upon us to love not only the virtuous and the wise but also the vicious and the stupid man. The rabbis have, indeed, interpreted the commandment to imply that even a criminal remains our neighbor.

The image-love is a love of what God loves, an act of sympathy, of participation in God's love. It is unconditional and regardless of man's merits or distinctions.

According to many thinkers, love is induced by that which delights or commands admiration. Such a view would restrict love to those worthy of receiving it and condition it upon whether a person might invoke delight or admiration. It would exclude the criminal and the corrupt members of society. In contrast, to love man, according to Judaism, is not a response to any physical, intellectual, or moral value of a person. We must love man because he is made in the image of God. "Said Rabbi Akiva: *Love thy neighbor as thyself* is the supreme principle of the Torah. You must not say, since I have been put to shame (by a fellow man), let him be put to shame; since I have been slighted, let him be slighted. Said Rabbi Tanhuma: If you do so, know whom you put to shame, for in the likeness of God made He him."

Thus God loves Israel notwithstanding its backslidings (Hos. 11:1f). His love is a gift rather than an earning (Hos. 14:5). "It is not because you are the most numerous of peoples that the Lord set His heart on you and chose you—indeed you are the smallest of peoples, but it was because the Lord loved you ..." (Deut. 7:7–8).

Sparingly does the term "image of God" occur in the Bible. Beyond the first chapter of Genesis, it comes forth in two instances: to remind us that everything found on earth was placed under the dominion of man, except human life, and to remind us that the body of man, not only his soul, is endowed with divine dignity.

The image of God is employed in stressing the criminality of murder. "For your life-blood, too, I will require a reckoning: of every beast will I require it; of man, too, will I require a reckoning for human life, of every man for that of his fellow man! Whoever sheds the blood of man, by man shall his blood be shed; for in the image of God was man created."

The image of man is also referred to in urging respect for the body of a criminal following his execution. "If a man has committed a crime punishable by death and he is put to death, and you hang him on a tree, his body shall not remain all night upon the tree, but you shall bury him the same day, for the dignity (or glory) of God is hanged (on the tree)."

The intention of the verse is stressed boldly by Rabbi Meir, an outstanding authority of the second century of the common era, in the form of a parable. "To what may this be compared? To twin brothers who lived in one city; one was appointed king, and the other took to highway robbery. At the king's command they hanged him. But all who saw him exclaimed: The king is hanged! (for being twins their appearance was similar.) Whereupon the king issued a command and he was taken down."

Great, therefore, must be our esteem for every man. "Let the honor of your disciple be as dear to you as your own, let the regard for your colleague be like the reverence due to your teacher, and let the reverence for your teacher be like the reverence for God." From this statement, a medieval authority concludes that our esteem for man must be as great as our esteem for God.

The divine likeness of man is an idea known in many religions. It is the contribution of Judaism to have taught the tremendous implication of that idea: the metaphysical dignity of man, the divine preciousness of human life. Man is not valued in physical terms; his value is infinite. To our common sense, one human being is less than two human beings. Jewish tradition tries to teach us that for him who has caused a single soul to perish, it is as though he had caused a whole world to perish; and that for him who has saved a single soul, it is as though he has saved a whole world. This thought was conveyed in the solemn admonition to witnesses not by false testimony to be the cause of the death of an innocent man.

No person may be sacrificed to save others. "If an enemy said to a group of women, 'Give us one from among you that we may defile her, and if not we will defile you all,' let the enemy defile them all, but let them not betray to them one single soul."

The transcendent dignity of man implies not only inalienable rights but also incredible responsibility. Stressing the idea that one man came to be the father of all men, the Mishnah avers: "Therefore every man is bound to say, 'On account of *me* the world was created.'" That is, every man is to regard himself as precious as a whole world, too precious to be wasted by sin.

When the Roman government issued a decree that the Jews of Palestine should not study the Torah, should not circumcise their sons and should profane the Sabbath, the Jewish leaders went to Rome and marched through the streets at night-time, proclaiming: "Alas, in heaven's name, are we not your brothers, are we not the sons of one father and the sons of one mother? Why are we different from every nation and tongue that you issue such harsh decrees against us?"

"Why was only a single man created? To teach you that for him who destroys one man, it is regarded as if he had destroyed all men, and that for him who saves one man, it is regarded as though he had saved all men. Furthermore, it was for the sake of peace, so that man might not say to his fellow man, 'My father was greater than thy father.'"

The awareness of divine dignity must determine even man's relation to his own self. His soul as well as his body constitutes an image of God. This is why one is under obligation to keep his body clean. "One must wash his face, hands, and feet daily in his Maker's honor." Hillel, it is said, explained this obligation by a parable. Those who are in charge of the icons of kings which are set up in their theaters and circuses scour and wash them off, and are rewarded and honored for so doing; how much more, who was created in the image and likeness of God.

Indeed, Jewish piety may be expressed in the form of a supreme imperative: *Treat thyself as an image of God.* It is in the light of this imperative that we can understand the meaning of the astonishing commandment: "You shall be holy, for I, the Lord your God, am holy" (Lev. 19:2). Holiness, an essential attribute of God, may become a quality of man. The human can become holy.[1]

Primary Sources

INTRODUCTION

The ethics of Judaism is dominated by the principle of universalism, in other words, in its demands and precepts it knows no difference between Jews and non-Jews. What it commands applies to everyone: the division of human beings by descent and faith is insignificant for it. To assume that it makes the commandments of justice, truth and love more binding on Jews acting among themselves than where the claims of those of other faiths require attention would be not only to devalue the Jewish doctrine of morality but completely to misunderstand it.

As with moral obligation, so too in respect of an aptitude for morality Judaism makes no distinction between human beings. The human being as such is both an object and a subject of morality. All the children of the earth are at the same time children of God, capable of doing good and called to do it, increasingly consolidating God's rule in the world. A moral disposition is innate in all human beings, and it depends on them to develop it into an ever greater power in the fight with their impulses and desires.

The Jewish doctrine of the Messiah, that future hope which at its highest level, under the image of the kingdom of God on earth, sees the moral quality of peoples and nations as the final goal of the development of humankind, has become the grandiose expression of this view of the moral calling of all human beings.

On closer examination, the notion of the election of Israel, which at first glance seems to contradict the doctrine of the equal moral value of all human beings, is ordered, rather, under the fact that Israel—and this is the deepest sense of God's gracious action towards it—has the task of influencing the rest of humankind by giving it an example: it is not to preserve its ethical good for itself but to communicate it to all nations, so that they rise to an ever higher moral status.

Judaism is so far removed from making the moral worth dependent on the exercise of its ceremonial commandments that it promises the pious, i.e. the morally good among all peoples, a share in the eternal blessedness. For this reason it has also dispensed with a large-scale propaganda of conversion, although it does not refuse a welcome to the proselyte who comes voluntarily and without ulterior motives. The lack of real mission in Judaism in the last two millennia does not mean that Judaism does not trust the power of its own faith to attract converts, but corresponds to the conviction that the fulfillment of ethical demands is also possible outside its circle.[2]

Samson Hochfeld

And God said, "Let us make man in our image, after our likeness. They shall rule the fish of the sea, the birds of the sky, the cattle, the whole earth, and all the creeping things that creep on earth."

Genesis 1:26

You shall not take vengeance or bear a grudge against your countrymen. Love your fellow as yourself: I am the Lord.

Leviticus 19:18

When a stranger resides with you in your land, you shall not wrong him. The stranger who resides with you shall be to you as one of your citizens; you shall love him as yourself, for you were strangers in the land of Egypt: I the Lord am your God.

Leviticus 19:33–34

You shall have one standard for stranger and citizen alike: for I the Lord am your God.

Leviticus 24:22

If your kinsman, being in straits, comes under your authority, and you hold him as though a resident alien, let him live by your side: do not exact from him advance or accrued interest, but fear your God. Let him live by your side as your kinsman.

Leviticus 25:35–36

⌁

It is to share your bread with the hungry,
And to take the wretched poor into your home;
When you see the naked, to clothe him,
And not to ignore your own kin.
Then shall your light burst through like the dawn
And your healing spring up quickly;
Your Vindicator shall march before you,
The Presence of the Lord shall be your rear guard.

Isaiah 58:7–8

⌁

What is man that You have been mindful of him, mortal man that You have taken note of him, that You have made him little less than divine, and adored him with glory and majesty?

Psalm 8:5–6

⌁

The term murder or manslaughter is used to signify the act of one who has killed a human being, but in real truth that act is a sacrilege, and the worst of sacrileges; seeing that of all the treasures which the universe has in its store there is none more sacred and godlike than man, the glorious cast of a glorious image, shaped according to the pattern of the archetypal form of the Word.[3]

Philo of Alexandria

⌁

A third reason is that He wills that no king or despot swollen with arrogance and contempt should despise an insignificant private person but should study in the school of the divine laws and abate his supercilious airs, and through the reasonableness or rather the assured truth of their arguments unlearn his self-conceit. For if the Uncreated, the Incorruptible, the Eternal, Who needs nothing and is the maker of all, the Benefactor and King of kings and God of gods could not brook to despise even the humblest, but designed to banquet him on holy oracles and statutes, as though he should be the sole guest, as though for him alone the feast was prepared to give good cheer to a soul instructed in the holy secrets and accepted for admission to the greatest mysteries, what right have I, the mortal, to bear myself proud-necked, puffed-up and loud-voiced, towards my fellows, who, though their fortunes be unequal, have equal rights of kinship because they can claim to be children of the one common mother of mankind, nature?[4]

Philo of Alexandria

∾

For a man stamps many coins with the one seal and they are all like one another; but the King of kings, the Holy One, blessed is He, has stamped every man with the seal of the first man, yet not one of them is like his fellow. Therefore every one must say, For my sake was the world created.[5]   Mishnah Sanhedrin *4:5*

∾

Therefore but a single man was created in the world, to teach that if any man has caused a single soul to perish from Israel Scripture imputes it to him as though he had caused a whole world to perish; and if any man saves alive a single soul from Israel Scripture imputes it to him as though he has saved alive a whole world. Again [but a single man was created] for the sake of peace among mankind, that none should say to his fellow, "My father was greater than thy father."[6]   Mishnah Sanhedrin *4:5*

∾

A favorite saying of the Rabbis of Jabneh was: I am God's creature and my fellow is God's creature. My work is in the town and his work is in the country. I rise early for my work and he rises early for his work. Just as he does not presume to do my work, so I do not presume to do his work. Will you say, I do much and he does little? We have learnt: One may do much or one may do little; it is all one, provided he directs his heart to heaven.

Babylonian Talmud, Berakhot 17a

❧

R. Hama son of R. Haninah further said: What means the text, *Ye shall walk after the Lord your God?* Is it, then, possible for a human being to walk after the *Shechinah* [God's presence]; for has it not been said, *For the Lord thy God is a devouring fire?* But [the meaning is] to walk after the attributes of the Holy One, blessed be He. As He clothes the naked, for it is written, *And the Lord God made for Adam and for his wife coats of skin, and clothed them,* so do thou also clothe the naked. The Holy One, blessed be He, visited the sick, for it is written, *And the Lord appeared unto him by the oaks of Mamre,* so do thou also visit the sick. The Holy One, blessed be He, comforted mourners, for it is written, *And it came to pass after the death of Abraham, that God blessed Isaac his son,* so do thou also comfort mourners. The Holy One, blessed be He, buried the dead, for it is written, *And He buried him in the valley,* so do thou also bury the dead.... R. Simlai expounded: Torah begins with an act of benevolence and ends with an act of benevolence. It begins with an act of benevolence, for it is written, *And the Lord God made for Adam and for his wife coats of skin, and clothed them;* and it ends with an act of benevolence, for it is written, *And He buried him in the valley.*

Babylonian Talmud, Sotah 14a

❧

The poor of the heathen are not prevented from gathering gleanings, forgotten sheaves and the corner of the field, to avoid ill feeling. Our Rabbis have taught: "We support the poor of the heathen along with the poor of Israel, and visit the sick of the heathen along with the sick of Israel, and bury the poor of the heathen along with the dead of Israel, in the interests of peace."

Babylonian Talmud, Gittin 61a

When a man is asked in the world-to-come: "What was thy work?" and he answers: "I fed the hungry," it will be said to him: "*This is the gate of the Lord* (Ps. 118:20). Enter into it, O thou that didst feed the hungry." When a man answers: "I gave drink to the thirsty," it will be said to him: "*This is the gate of the Lord.* Enter into it, O thou that didst give drink to the thirsty." When a man answers: "I clothed the naked," it will be said to him: "*This is the gate of the Lord.* Enter into it, O thou that didst clothe the naked." This will be said also to him that brought up the fatherless, and to them that gave alms or performed deeds of loving-kindness.[7]

Midrash Tehillim on Psalm 118:17

Scripture says, "You shall keep my laws and my rules … by the pursuit of which man shall live": R. Jeremiah says, "How do I know that even a gentile who keeps the Torah, lo, he is like the high priest?" "Scripture says, 'by the pursuit of which man shall live.'" And so he says, "'And this is the Torah of the priests, Levites, and Israelites,' is not what is said here, but rather, 'This is the Torah of the man, O Lord God' (2 Sam. 7:19)." And so he says, "'Open the gates and let priests, Levites, and Israelites enter it' is not what is said, but rather, 'Open the gates and let the righteous nation, who keeps faith, enter it' (Isa. 26:2)." And so he says, "'This is the gate of the Lord. Priests, Levites, and Israelites …' is not what is said, but rather, 'the righteous shall enter into it' (Ps. 118:20)." And so he says, "What is said is not, 'Rejoice, priests, Levites, and Israelites,' but rather, 'Rejoice, O righteous, in the Lord' (Ps. 33:1)." And so he says, "It is not, 'Do good, O Lord, to the priests, Levites, and Israelites,' but rather, 'Do good, O Lord, to the good, to the upright in heart' (Ps. 125:4)." "Thus, even a gentile who keeps the Torah, lo, he is like the high priest."[8]

Midrash Sifra to Leviticus 18:5

~

With regard to moral conduct, the principle that a man must always act benevolently toward his neighbor and never cause him harm, applies to his neighbor's body, possessions, and feelings.[9]

Moses Hayyim Luzzatto

~

Who has a wise head? He who learns from everyone! This means that each should also find his own errors in each of his neighbor's errors.[10]

Baal Shem Tov

~

Three times the Torah asks us to love: twice, in Leviticus (19:18, 34), we are commanded to love human beings; then, in Deuteronomy, our love is directed toward God. Only after we have learned to love people can we come to love God.[11]

Chasidic

~

But all men are created in the image of God, not the progenitor of one nation or another exclusively, but the progenitor of all, and from him the whole human race have descended *vested with equal rights.*[12]

Abraham Geiger

~

Take the stranger. Trustful does he enter your country, your city, your community, confident of finding people who will respect him as their fellow-man and not begrudge him a place among themselves where he can live, and live like a human being; he has no other letter of recommendation than his human countenance, nobody to introduce him but God, Who presents him to you as His child, and says: "He is like you, may he do as you do—grant him equal rights—he is My child, My earth is his home; I have called on him, just as I called on you, joyfully to fulfill his task as a human being; do not curtail that right of his, do not spoil his joy of life, do not abuse his helplessness; show that you feel that your soil is God's soil, and that man is God's child." Though others may discriminate against the Jew and not recognize you, the "stranger" as a human being—you, as a Jew, a son of Israel, must not fail to recognize every stranger as a human being! In *Mitzrayim* you learned that God protects the stranger.[13]

Samson Raphael Hirsch

So God already set human beings apart at creation, raised above the series of natural beings; for in the human being there is a divine breath, the human being is not a creature of earth, he is an image of God. Thus God has chosen him—not merely this human being or that, not this people or that, not Assur, not Egypt, nor even Israel, but simply mortal, frail man. And for what is this man chosen, recognized as worthy, destined? Merely to serve God. The [eighth] psalm emphasized the dignity of the human being as ruler; here [in a prayer for the conclusion of the Day of Atonement] it is the priestly dignity of the human being which is regarded as his destiny and which *exalts* him *above* all nature, though he stands *within it* in precisely the same way as the animal.[14]

Heymann Steinthal

Judaism obligates those who confess it to show neighborly love to every human being as such and prohibits retribution of injustice suffered against any human being as such, because the human being is the image of God or because the human being is related to his neighbor as one of his hands to the other.[15]

Moritz Güdemann

We turn now to the political antinomy between Israel and the foreigner. We have already encountered the necessity that the mission of monotheism imposed on humanity, namely, that this mission required the destruction of polytheism, which destruction in turn entailed the destruction of idolatrous peoples. This anomaly can be resolved only on the basis of historical considerations. The share of religion in reason retreats in this case before the logic of facts, a logic that cannot hold its own before pure ethics. Can one, however, ask why God did not arrange it, did not command it, differently? Theodicy becomes absurdity in the case of this question. We therefore have to disregard this anomaly and, despite its contradictory character, attempt a conciliation.

Although the worshipers of idols have to be fought no less in one's own people than in the alien peoples, it nevertheless says: "Thou shalt not abhor an Edomite, for he is thy brother." This is one of the golden sentences in support of neighborly love: the Edomite, this enemy of Israel, is called "brother." Consequently not only is the Israelite a brother, but even the hostile worshiper of idols is called the same. Then it is no wonder that this prohibition is also extended to the Egyptian: "Thou shalt not abhor an Egyptian." And the four hundred years of slavery are not recalled there; rather, there this thought is emphasized: "because thou wast a stranger in his land" (Deut. 23:8). The stranger is not thought of as a slave, but as a guest-friend, who requires the piety of guest-friendship. Humanity is already so rooted in the stranger that the slave, as stranger, can be admonished to the bond of gratitude.... Thus, man is also recognized in the *non-Israelite*, and this recognition is also confirmed by a political acknowledgment of him. The blemish of idol worship is thus separated, if not from the concept, at least from the representation of man. Man need not be an Israelite in order not to have to be a worshipper of idols.... The more striking, therefore, is the purely moral share of reason in monotheism, as seen in the literary fact that monotheism made the foreigner into fellowman, even without his joining the monotheistic religion. And this consideration is the more important as it is actualized in the realm of politics.[16]

Hermann Cohen

❧

Social life, therefore, must be built upon the firm foundation of justice, the full recognition of the rights of all individuals and all classes. It can be based neither upon the formal administration of law nor upon the elastic principle of love, which too often tolerates, or even approves certain types of injustice.[17]

Kaufmann Kohler

❧

In so-called "Mosaism" the religious and moral situation has intrinsically grown up with the state social system. The basic dogmas of faith are presented as guiding principles for practical life. Thus for example, transferred to social life, the exalted principle of the one and only God produces the *principle of the equality* of all men before this sole supreme power, a principle on which the whole of biblical legislation is built. The commandments to love one's neighbor, the contempt for slavery, the obligation to support the power, the humane treatment of foreigners, compassion and mercy for all living creatures—all these exalted laws are the direct consequence of that principle of equality. The biblical legislation offers perhaps the only example of an order of state and society which is based not only on the abstractions of the mind but also the demands of feeling and the noblest stirrings of the human soul. Alongside the principle of formal right and law it brings out the principle of justice and humanity and embodies it in a whole series of precepts. The Mosaic law is a "propaganda of action": it requires everywhere an active, not merely a passive, morality.[18]

Simon Dubnow

❧

However great the differences among men, their likeness to God is common to all of them, and it is this likeness which establishes the human in man. God's covenant was made with all human beings. Not this or that individual but every man was created in the image of God; for therein lies the meaning of all human life. To say that every human being is "a child of God" (Deut. 14:1) is another biblical expression for the idea that every man was created in His image. What is most important to humanity is contained equally in all men. Place and task are assigned to all and human nobility resides in all. To deny it to one would be to deny it to all. Above delimitations of race and nation, of caste and class, of masters and servants, and of talents and powers stands the certainty: "man." Whoever bears the human visage was created and called to be a revelation of human dignity.[19]

Leo Baeck

The recognition which we owe our fellow man is therefore absolute and unlimited; for it is based on the fact that he is a being of my being with a dignity like unto mine. The command in Leviticus, which Akiva called the determining sentence of the Bible, and which is usually rendered, "Love thy neighbor as thyself" (Lev. 19:18), means in its truest sense, love thy neighbor for he is as thou. This "as thou" is the essence of the sentence. For Judaism this utterance is neither mere philosophy nor sentimental enthusiasm, but an unqualified commandment to honor our fellow man who is as we are. Not because he achieves this or that are we to respect him, but simply because he is a man.[20]

Leo Baeck

Judaism did not succumb to that narrowness of religious conception which proclaims salvation as the monopoly of one church. Where the deed rather than belief leads to God; where the community offers its members an ideal and a task as spiritual symbols of their participation, there mere belief cannot of itself guarantee the salvation of the soul. And likewise the loss of salvation cannot depend on the accident of birth which causes a human being to belong to a different religious group. Throughout the Bible one finds traces, faint but distinct, of the doctrine that all men seek God: "from the rising of the sun even unto the going down thereof the Lord's name is praised" (Mal. 1:11; Ps. 113:3). Even the heathen try to be pious; they too find a way to attain divine forgiveness for their sins. One contrast becomes increasingly decisive: that between God-fearing and godless. And "God-fearing," in the true meaning of the word, applies to every person who believes in the One God and does right. Such words of quality as *"hasid"* (pious) or *"zaddik"* (righteous), intended to describe the best among the Jews, are soon applied also to the heathen, until the moral equality of all men finds its classical expression in the sentence: "The pious of all nations will have a share in the life to come." One need but compare this conception with Dante's description of the place of expiation in which even the best of heathen face ghastly doom—a description in accordance with the basic teachings of the Church—in order to see the contrast at its most vivid.[21]   *Leo Baeck*

When I confront a human being as my You and speak the basic word I-You to him, then he is no thing among things nor does he consist of things.

He is no longer He or She, limited by other Hes and Shes, a dot in the world grid of space and time, nor a condition that can be experienced and described, a loose bundle of named qualities. Neighborless and seamless, he is You and fills the firmament. Not as if there were nothing but he; but everything else lives in *his* light.

Even as a melody is not composed of tones, nor a verse of words, nor a statue of lines—one must pull and tear to turn a unity into a multiplicity—so it is with the human being to whom

I say You. I can abstract from him the color of his hair or the color of his speech or the color of his graciousness; I have to do this again and again; but immediately he is no longer You.

And even as prayer is not in time but time in prayer, the sacrifice not in space but space in the sacrifice—and whoever reverses the relation annuls the reality—I do not find the human being to whom I say You in any Sometime and Somewhere. I can place him there and have to do this again and again, but immediately he becomes a He or a She, an It, and no longer remains my You.

As long as the firmament of the You is spread over me, the tempests of causality cower at my heels, and the whirl of doom congeals.

The human being to whom I say You I do not experience. But I stand in relation to him, in the sacred basic word. Only when I step out of this do I experience him again. Experience is remoteness from You.

The relation can obtain even if the human being to whom I say You does not hear it in his experience. For You is more than It knows. You does more, and more happens to it, than It knows. No deception reaches this far: here is the cradle of actual life.[22]

Martin Buber

Core Ethic 2

The golden rule: do not do to another what you would not want to be done to you.

Love of Neighbor

Samson Hochfeld

The creative achievements of Judaism include the discovery of the fellow human being and thus of humankind. The concern of the non-Jewish thinker of antiquity is concentrated on the self, and the weal and woe of the other is asked after only incidentally. What is the goal of human life? This is the basic problem of ethics for the Greek philosophers. Happiness, is their answer, and depending on their standpoint each indicates different ways of attaining this happiness: the control of the impulses by reason, enjoyment, a lack of needs, relaxation. Not a single one of them has found the answer: you shall be happy by making your fellow human beings happy, by showing them good, by helping them, by easing the burden of their lives. With few exceptions, the non-Jewish ethics of antiquity has an egotistic orientation; it is an individual ethics, to which the great questions of social ethics remain alien. But the Bible has introduced the fellow human being into ethical consideration and elevated his well-being to be a norm for judging human action.

For according to the biblical view the human being is not an individual being who exists in isolation and may oppress and exploit other human beings to achieve his personal satisfaction; rather, he is a member of a totality that consists of individuals with equal rights and equal obligations. The totality is to be preserved, to grow and flourish and rise to ever higher levels of power and achievement. Every individual is to take part in this work in the service of the totality and to receive his human worth from it. Depending on his gifts and disposition he is assigned a higher or lower place for his activity in the organism of the whole, but no one is excluded or so unusable that he can be dispensed with.

From here we understand the role played by justice and love in Jewish ethics. Justice makes itself known generally in behavior that avoids or guards against invasions of the living space of others, love in the desire to promote the life of others. There cannot be a totality of human beings without justice *and* love. The former marks out the capacities of the individual members from one another, the latter intervenes when the demarcation leads to harshness; the one is the substructure on which the community securely rests, the other is the mortar which holds together the stones and walls. According to the Jewish understanding, justice and love belong together like rain and sunshine in the growth of plants or like the male and female elements in marriage. The close connection with love has preserved Jewish justice from doing supreme injustice, *summa iniuria*, from degenerating into a rigid principle, lifeless formalism; but the abiding contact with justice has protected Jewish love from losing itself by wallowing in feelings and leaving out of account the real conditions of life.

Love of neighbor, which accordingly has the task of mitigating and relieving, of supporting and standing by, of comforting and helping, in a word in making possible for others a human life, a life in the framework and service of the totality, embraces the whole scale of relationships in which human beings can stand to one another; it extends from the acquaintance and friend through the fellow-citizen and fellow-countryman to the unknown member of an alien race and a distant land. The fact that he has a human face makes everyone appear worthy of this love. Nor does love of neighbor stop at the differences which have created success and failure, wealth and poverty, superfluity and need; just as it expresses itself there as philanthropy and a benevolent disposition free of envy, so it expresses itself here as mercy, gentleness and care of the poor; it rises in accordance with the needs of the hour from the small favor to the generous act of help, from the occasional gift to sacrificial surrender.

In its effort to span all conditions of life and do right with its help, Jewish love of neighbor has established a principle which always proves fruitful and can be followed everywhere: put yourself in the position of the other, then judge and act! If you come face to face with an unknown person who needs you, reflect how he can be encouraged. Approach an unfortunate person who has transgressed, note the circumstances in which he has been driven from the way. If you are in doubt about the motives which have been at work in the life of the other which has gone wrong, judge according to the favorable aspect. This invitation to put oneself in the situation, the mood, the mentality of the other comes into play in the tenderest way in the regulation of the relationship between master and servant: Judaism commands that one should not make the one who serves feel his subordinate position, but rule over him with gentleness; one should not expect of him anything that violates his humanity.

The attitude of Judaism to the problem of love of enemy, or the question of the permissibility of personal revenge connected with it, deserves a separate account. While the saying attributed to our Bible, "You shall hate your enemy," cannot be found in it, defence against groundless attacks, the fight against lawbreaking and disturbing the peace can. To hand oneself over with no will of one's own to the enemy would mean to strengthen him in his will to annihilate; to grant free scope to violence would mean to endanger the existence of human fellowship. Therefore if defence is ethically justified, vengeance goes beyond what is permissible and necessary. To store up resentment in order to pay back what one has suffered, to recompense evil with evil, is not just a sin against the other but also sin against his own human dignity. That is the core of the *Jewish* commandment to love one's enemy: the enemy too is and remains a human being, however much he may have denied his humanity. If he is in need you should be able to forget and not refuse him your help; but you should never allow yourself to follow his example and thus humiliate yourself.

According to Jewish teaching, to be able to forget, forgive and practice reconciliation for the sake of the human being and humankind is the highest, finest and most effective means of safeguarding the existence of the totality. Were all insults, offences and hurts kept in mind and responded to on occasion, there would be a war of all against all, and a life in community would be impossible. Only by aligning one's person and its interests to the whole of humankind and becoming subordinate to it, and seeing the purpose and reward of one's own efforts in the flourishing of the totality, does one gain the power to overcome oneself and dispense not only with satisfying vain wishes but even with implementing perhaps legitimate demands. Therefore with this eye on the totality Judaism has on the one hand prescribed that strife should be avoided and where it has already broken out it should be settled as soon as possible; on the other hand it has praised the increasing of harmony among men as the supreme merit. Judaism crowns its commandment to love one's neighbor with admonitions to bring together again those who have become alienated, settle disputes between others by removing misunderstandings and dissipating annoyances and preparing a lasting home for peace on earth.[1]

Primary Sources

INTRODUCTION

In the commandment, this something is designated as the neighbor. More precisely the word designates, in the Hebrew original as well as in Greek, the *nearest* neighbor precisely at the moment of love, the one who is nighest to me, at least at this moment, regardless of what he may have been before or will be afterward. Thus the neighbor is only a representative. He is not loved for his own sake, nor for his beautiful eyes, but only because he just happens to be standing there, because he happens to be nighest to me. Another could as easily stand in his place—precisely at this place nearest me. The neighbor is the other, the *plesios* of the Septuagint, the *plesios allos* of Homer. Thus the neighbor is, as stated, only *locum tenens*. Love goes out to whatever is nighest to it as to a representative, in the fleeting moment of its presentness, and thereby in truth to the all-inclusive concept of all men and all things which could ever assume this place of being its highest neighbor. In the final analysis it goes out to everything, to the world....

Man's act of love is, after all, only apparently an act. He is not told by God to do unto his neighbor as he would be dealt with himself. This is the practical form of the commandment to love one's neighbor, for use as a rule of conduct. Actually it merely designates the lower negative limit; it forbids the transgression of this limit in conduct. For this reason even its external form is better phrased in the negative. Rather, man is to love his neighbor like himself. Like himself. Your neighbor is "like thee." Man is not to deny himself. Precisely here in the commandment to love one's neighbor, his self is definitely confirmed in its place. The world is not thrown in his face as an endless melee, nor is he told, while a finger points to the whole melee: that is you. That is you—therefore stop distinguishing yourself from it, penetrate it, dissolve in it, lose yourself in it. No, it is quite different. Out of the endless chaos of the world, one nighest thing, his neighbor, is placed before his soul, and concerning this one and well-nigh only concerning this one he is told: he is like you. "Like you," and thus not "you." You remain You and you are to remain just that. But he is not to remain a He for you, and thus a mere It for your You. Rather he is like You, like your You, a You like You, an I—a soul....

Man's eternity is implanted in the soil of creation. Being loved and loving are the two moments of his life, separate before God, yet united in man, and creation would be the And between them. Being loved comes to man from God, loving turns toward the world. How else could they count as one for him? How else could he be conscious of loving God by loving his neighbor if he did not know from the first and the innermost that the neighbor is God's creature and that his love of neighbor is love of the creatures. And how could he be conscious of being loved by God other than as the equal of him whom he himself loves in the neighbor; how else than because God has created in his image that which is common to him and his neighbor, namely the fact that the latter is "like him" so that both "are men." He is the creature of God and the image of God, and this is the foundation, laid down from creation, on which he can build the house of his eternal life in the temporal cross-currents of love of God and love of neighbor.[2]

Franz Rosenzweig

When you encounter your enemy's ox or ass wandering, you must take it back to him. When you see the ass of your enemy lying under its burden and would refrain from raising it, you must nevertheless raise it with him.

Exodus 23:4–5

Love your fellow as yourself: I am the Lord.

Leviticus 19:18

⌒

If your enemy falls, do not exult; if he trips, let your heart not rejoice.   *Proverbs 24:17*

⌒

If your enemy is hungry, give him bread to eat; if he is thirsty, give him water to drink.   *Proverbs 25:21*

⌒

Take heed to thyself, my child, in all thy works, and be discreet in all thy behavior. And what thou thyself hatest, do to no man.
                                                                    Tobit 4:14–15

⌒

And let your mind be unto good, even as ye know me; for he that hath his mind right seeth all things rightly. Fear ye the Lord, and love your neighbor.
                                    Testaments of the Twelve Patriarchs 12:3

⌒

On another occasion it happened that a certain heathen came before Shammai and said to him, "Make me a proselyte, on condition that you teach me the whole Torah while I stand on one foot." Thereupon he repulsed him with the builder's cubit which was in his hand. When he went before Hillel, he said to him, "What is hateful to you, do not to your neighbor: that is the whole Torah, while the rest is the commentary thereof; go and learn it."
                                        Babylonian Talmud, Shabbat 31a

⌒

One day he [R. Johanan] was journeying on the road and he saw a man planting a carob tree; he asked him, How long does it take [for this tree] to bear fruit? The man replied: Seventy years. He then further asked him: Are you certain that you will live another

seventy years? The man replied: I found [ready grown] carob trees in the world; as my forefathers planted these for me so I too plant these for my children.
Babylonian Talmud, Taanit 23a

~

Resh Lakish said: Whoever wrests the judgment of the proselyte is as if he wrests the judgment of the All-High, for it is said: *And that turn aside the proselyte from his right*: the consonants [can be read]: *And that turn Me aside*.
Babylonian Talmud, Chagigah 5a

~

In the measure with which a man measures it is meted out to him.
Babylonian Talmud, Sotah 8b

~

Hillel said, "Don't separate yourself from the community. Don't be overconfident until the day of your death. Don't judge your fellow human being until you have reached that person's place. Don't say anything that is unintelligible with the hope that it will be understood. And don't say, 'When I have leisure, I will study'— perhaps, you never will have that leisure."
Pirke Avot/Sayings of the Fathers 2:4

~

Rabbi Eliezer said, "Let your friend's honor be as precious to you as your own. Be difficult to provoke. And repent one day before your death."
Pirke Avot/Sayings of the Fathers 2:10

~

Rabbi Yose would say, "Let your friend's property be as dear to you as your own. Since you cannot inherit the Torah, you must prepare yourself to study it. Let all that you do be for the sake of Heaven."
Pirke Avot/Sayings of the Fathers 2:12

~

Ben Azzai would say, "Run to do the least of the commandments as you would to do the most important. Run away from a transgression, for a commandment pulls along a commandment and a transgression pulls along a transgression. The reward of a commandment is a commandment and the reward of a transgression is a transgression."

Pirke Avot/Sayings of the Fathers 4:2

Rabbi Elazar ben Shammua would say, "Let the honor of your student be as dear to you as your own. Let the honor of your associate be equal to the respect due to your teacher. Let the respect due to your teacher be equivalent to the reverence due to Heaven."

Pirke Avot/Sayings of the Fathers 4:12

It is related that an ass-driver came to R. Akiva and said to him, "Rabbi, teach me the whole Torah all at once." He replied, "My son, Moses our teacher stayed on the Mount forty days and forty nights before he learned it, and you want me to teach you the whole of it at once! Still, my son, this is the basic principle of the Torah: What is hateful to yourself, do not to your fellow-man. If you wish that nobody should harm you in connection with what belongs to you, you must not harm him in that way; if you wish that nobody should take away from you what is yours, do not take away from another what is his." The man rejoined his companions, and they journeyed until they came to a field full of seed-pods. His companions each took two, but he took none. They continued their journey, and came to a field full of cabbages. They each took two, but he took none. They asked him why he had not taken any, and he replied, "Thus did R. Akiva teach me: What is hateful to yourself, do not to your fellow-man. If you wish that nobody should take from you what is yours, do not take from another what is his."[3]

Avot de Rabbi Natan

Rabbi Joshua says: A grudging eye, evil impulse, and hatred of mankind put a man out of the world. [*Pirke Avot* 2:11]. A grudging eye: what is that? This teaches that even as a man looks out for his own home, so should he look out for the home of his fellow. And even as no man wishes that his own wife and children be held in ill repute, so should no man wish that his fellow's wife and his fellow's children be held in ill repute.[4]

Avot de Rabbi Natan

A person should take account with his soul regarding his cooperation with his fellow-men in what affects the general welfare, such as ploughing and reaping, buying and selling, and other relations wherein human beings are mutually helpful in maintaining social existence. He should be happy in the thought that others have what he would love to have for himself. He should hate that anything should happen to others which he would hate happening to himself. He should feel compassion for others. He should do what is in his power to avert anything that would injure them.[5]

Bachya ben Joseph ibn Paquda

Do not accuse your neighbor of any failing which you yourself have.[6]

Rashi

The goal for which each human being should strive is first to improve his own qualities, and only then those of his neighbor.[7]

Moses ibn Ezra

Free Will is bestowed on every human being. If one desires to turn toward the good way and be righteous, he has the power to do so. If one wishes to turn towards the evil way and be wicked, he is at liberty to do so. And thus is it written in the Torah, "Behold, the man is become as one of us, to know good and evil" (Gen. 3:22)— which means that the human species had become unique in the world—there being no other species like it in the following respect, namely, that man, of himself and by the exercise of his own intelligence and reason, knows what is good and what is evil, and there is none who can prevent him from doing that which is good or that which is evil.... Let not the notion, expressed by foolish gentiles and most of the senseless folk among Israelites, pass through your mind that at the beginning of a person's existence, the Almighty decrees that he is to be either righteous or wicked. This is not so. Every human being may become righteous like Moses, our teacher, or wicked like Jerobeam; wise or foolish, merciful or cruel; niggardly or generous; and so with all other qualities. There is no one that coerces him or decrees what he is to do, or draws him to either of two ways; but every person turns to the way which he desires, spontaneously and of his own volition.... This doctrine is an important principle, the pillar of the Law and the Commandment.[8]

Moses Maimonides

A person ought to speak in praise of his neighbor and be careful of his neighbor's property as he is careful of his own property and solicitous about his own honor.[9]   *Moses Maimonides*

One must accept what is true and right in every human being, even though he is insignificant and even belongs to another people.[10]   *Jacob ben Abbamari*

The reason some prayers are unanswered is that the person who prays does not commiserate with his neighbor's pain and suffering. It stands to reason that his prayers are not answered because he should have considered, "If I were in his predicament, I would have prayed for relief." And it says, "Love your neighbor as you love yourself" (Lev. 19:18). Now, since he did not sympathize with his neighbor's plight, it is only fair that his prayers are not answered. That is why the Sages formulated all our prayers and supplications in the plural.[11]

Yehudah HeChasid

It enjoins upon us the love of mankind, "And thou shalt love thy neighbor as thyself." It forbids hatred, "Thou shalt not hate thy brother in thy heart." In respect to the stranger it says, "And ye shall love the stranger," and it admonishes us not to vex him, "He shall dwell with thee, in the midst of thee, in the place which he shall choose within one of thy gates, where it liketh him best; thou shalt not wrong him." And this applies not merely to a proselyte, but also to one who is not converted to Judaism, provided he does not worship idols.[12]

Joseph Albo

The duty of the upright man, whenever one asks him for advice, is to give whatever counsel he would adopt for himself, if he were similarly placed, and to be mindful only of the good of the one who consults him, and have no selfish purpose whatever, immediate or remote. In case such advice is likely to be injurious to him who gives it, he should, if he can, either state that fact frankly to the one who consults him, or keep away from the matter entirely and proffer no advice.[13]

Moses Hayyim Luzzatto

Sinners are mirrors. If we find errors in them we must note that they only reflected the evil in ourselves.[14]

Baal Shem Tov

Someone who does not know his own worth—how can he esti-
mate that of another?[15]   *Jaakob Jossef from Polonia*

～

But Judaism was destined not alone to introduce a new idea concerning God into the world, but also to dignify and ennoble all
human relations. The men who taught in ancient time, "The true
foundation and nerve of the Law is, whatever displeases thee do
not unto others; this is the essence and root of the Law, all the rest
is commentary, go and learn"; or, "Thou shalt love thy neighbor as
thyself; this is the great cardinal principle of the Law"; or, "This is
the Book of the generations of man," is a still greater principle,
conveying, as it does, the lesson, to be man, to recognize under all
circumstances all men as our peers—the Hillels, Akivas, Ben
Somas, who taught such lessons, are the great props and pillars of
Judaism, and we must well take to heart their words. Judaism, I
repeat, did not enter into this world to present it with a new idea
concerning God, but to purify all human relations as well as the
knowledge and appreciation of man.[16]

Abraham Geiger

～

To see in your fellow-man something else than merely your rival
for the acquisition of the good things of the earth, not to look
upon his good as an encroachment on yours, to let your neighbor
have the spot of earth on which God has set him—as He has set
you on yours—and even to let him prosper on it—all this amounts
merely to not hating him, not yet to loving him. To love your
neighbor means to see in him the one condition of your own existence, of your own welfare, of your fulfilling your mission as man
and Israelite, and so, in the desire for your own being and living,
to include the desire for your neighbor's also.[17]

Samson Raphael Hirsch

～

But when the prophet had recognized God as holy, the demand was given that the human being, likening himself to God, should be holy. And when it is said "Love your neighbor as yourself, I am the Eternal One," this means: as I the Eternal One love you and your neighbor in the same way as a father, so, imitating me, you should love your neighbor like yourself; do to him everything precisely as you would wish God should do to you. Thus love of neighbor is merely the consequence of the demand to be like God.[18]

Heymann Steinthal

⌣

Though the rule of action framed in precise words (in Talmudic parlance, the Halachah) be the element of immediate importance in all moral cognition and a will calculated to produce energetic action be the most sterling and valuable element in moral conduct, yet the perfect flower of morality is not unfolded without the liveliest stirring of the moral feelings.

"The All-merciful requires the heart," says the Talmud with emphasis. Cognition of the law and action in conformity with law should become a matter of the heart. Lawfulness as an ethical conviction means more than knowing the law with clear insight, more than bringing about its fulfillment with energy; it means embracing the law with emotion, and being animated with the longing to see the law attain to supremacy in the world and in ourselves, so that our whole life may be ordered, guided, and enriched by its fulfillment.[19]

Moritz Lazarus

⌣

Love God above all things and your fellow human being as yourself; that is demanded by both revealed doctrine and the moral law.[20]

Moses Bloch

⌣

Since love cannot be commanded except by the lover himself, therefore the love for man, in being commanded by God, is directly derived from the love for God. The love for God is to express itself in love for one's neighbor. It is for this reason that love of neighbor can and must be commanded. Love of neighbor originated in the mystery of the directed volition; it is distinguished from all ethical acts by the presupposition of being loved by God, a presupposition which becomes visible behind this origin only through the form of the commandment.[21]

Franz Rosenzweig

~

At the centre of the prophetic demands is the doctrine that all piety and pleasing God must begin with love of fellow human beings and work itself out again in that. Religion and morality, the way to God and the way to human beings, coincide, are regarded as one.[22]   *Max Wiener*

~

To know the nature of God means to the prophets to know that he is just and incorruptible; that he is merciful, gracious and long-suffering; that he tries the heart of man; and that he has destined man for the good. Through knowledge of God we thereby learn what man should be, through the Divine is revealed the human. The ways of the Lord are the ways which man should follow—" and they shall keep the way of the Lord, to do justice and judgment" (Gen. 18:19). Hence a prerequisite to the understanding of man is an understanding of what God gave to him and commands him to do; it means more specifically to comprehend that man was created to be just, good, and holy, as is the Lord his God. And thereby the revelation of God and the conception of human morality are knitted together into a unity. Through God we learn to understand ourselves and to become true men. "He hath shewed thee, O man, what is good" (Micah 6:8). God speaks to us of the good which, for the sake of our life, is demanded of us. To seek God is to strive for the good; to find God is to do good. Do God's bidding, say the prophets, and then you will know who he is.[23]

Leo Baeck

∾

These last commandments expressly extend the love for neighbor to the enemy. Since the duty of justice is absolute and includes our enemy, we are to help him when he needs our support. This duty to the enemy carries within it a severe tension.... This tension is overcome by the demand for justice. Even though the enemy is a foe of the commandment and therefore not a fellow man, I must not be like him; I must fulfill my life by the justice I mete out to others and thus also to my enemy. Since that duty is absolute and unconditional, my enemy, no matter how much he separates himself from me, is still bound to me in the unity of man and fellow man. Precisely in relation to him do we realize the full strength of the commandment of humanity. That is why, as an old law puts it, duty toward him takes precedence over duty toward a friend. To return evil for evil would mean to deny the commandment enjoined upon us; it would mean that justice was subject to the assumption of our infallibility in inflicting punishment.... With good reason do these conceptions all begin with the negative, "Thou shalt not." "Thou shalt not take revenge, thou shalt not retaliate" (Lev. 19:18). For only through the negative is the way opened to the positive. Do no wrong to an enemy—that is the beginning. From the definite negative follows the definite positive act. Only on this basis does the love of the enemy not evaporate into empty sentiment.[24]

Leo Baeck

∾

Rabbi Akiva said that the verse "Thou shalt love thy neighbor as thyself" (Lev. 19:18) contains a great principle of the Torah. Everyone knows this verse and agrees with Rabbi Akiva on the great significance Judaism attaches to loving your neighbor. Yet there are very few verses in Scripture that have been so misunderstood. Many sensitive souls have tormented themselves because they think the verse means we are obliged to love others as we love ourselves but, in their honesty, know that they cannot. How can love be commanded? A person can be ordered to do this or that, but love is an emotion and emotions cannot be forced. The very notion of a command in this instance implies that love is a matter of choice, not of feeling.

It is astonishing that this verse is so often quoted out of context. Let us read the entire passage, not simply a part of it: "Thou shalt not take vengeance nor bear any grudge against the children of thy people, but thou shalt love thy neighbor as thyself: I am the Lord." In other words, the verse means act lovingly toward others by not wishing them harm. If you take revenge or bear a grudge against your neighbor, you are not acting in a loving manner toward your neighbor. The verse is not a command to love spuriously. To attempt that is fraudulent. It is impossible to love everyone; obviously there are those whom we dislike, and, since the verse applies to everyone, there are also people we hardly know well enough to love or hate.

Furthermore, Biblical scholars have pointed out that the word *kamokha* from Leviticus, usually translated into English as "as thyself," does not qualify "love" but "thy neighbor." The meaning is not "love your neighbor as thyself," but rather "love him because he is as thyself," i.e., a human being like you, with the same needs, the same hopes, the same right to be treated fairly.

Consequently, the verse can be paraphrased as: "Do not act hatefully or vengefully toward others; rather, act lovingly because they are like you and I am the Lord who created both you and them." This does not make the command easy to follow, but at least it can be followed, whereas a command to love others as ourselves is impossible except, perhaps, for the greatest of saints.[25]

Louis Jacobs

Core Ethic 3

Peace: commitment to a
culture of nonviolence and
reverence for all life.

The Tent of Peace

Hermann Cohen

The passions have their common foundation in that mystery of the soul which is constituted by hatred. Neither psychology nor ethics has determined whether hatred is an original direction of consciousness, or merely a transformation of some other instinctual force. It is above all a question of whether hatred does not rather belong to the pathological sphere, and, growing out of it, masquerades as a kind of psychological normality.... What means does the peace of soul secure in order to root out hatred from the human heart? It is not enough to oppose human love to hatred. For the chapter on the teaching of virtue has to indicate practical means, which will smooth the path for the ways of virtue; it cannot be satisfied merely with theory; it must offer practical solutions for moral theory. Therefore, it would also be insufficient if another designation were attempted, if hatred were perhaps interpreted as envy. For in that case there would be no less difficulty involved in combating and destroying envy.

At this point, even without being guided by polemics, we are led by our own considerations to the problem of love of the enemy. The Old Testament does not contain this command, but it contains, in fundamental expressions, the prohibition of enmity, of hatred for men. In the first instance this prohibition is expressed in the prohibition of vengeance and resentment. Further, it is expressed in the prohibition of forbearing assistance to the enemy with regard to the preservation of his property (Exod. 23:5). Finally, it results from the fundamental regulation in the prohibition: "Thou shalt not hate thy brother in thy heart" (Lev. 19:17). In this verse hatred is determined as opposition to the brother and to the heart, hence as opposition to the fellowman and to man's own foundation, which lies in his heart. The only question remains: through what practical means of virtue can this fundamental regulation be realized and hatred rooted out of the human heart?

The wisdom of the Talmud has progressed beyond the Bible. The Bible, in the psalms, knows only the false, the wrong hatred and the false enemies (Ps. 38:20; 35:19; 69:5). In all these verses the cause of hatred is called false; it remains possible that there could be a true cause of hatred.... The Talmud has discovered the concept of "wanton hatred" and introduced it into the prayers. Not only should hatred not have a false cause, but it has no cause at all. Any cause for hatred is empty and vain. Hatred is always wanton hatred. This is the deep wisdom which excels all love of the enemy and which first secures and psychologically strengthens human love. It is not enough that I recognize that I ought to love my enemy—apart from the fundamental question of whether both concepts are compatible. I can remove hatred from the human heart only insofar as I do not know any enemy at all; the information and the knowledge that a man is my enemy, that he hates me, must be as incomprehensible to me as that I myself could hate a man, and therefore it must drop out of my consciousness. The one must become as unintelligible to me as the other. People persuade themselves that they hate one another, but this is their delusion, the fateful outcome of their ignorance about their own soul and their consciousness. The vanity which Koheleth ascribes to everything is in this case related to hatred, and this vanity is expressed by a word which means futile, and that which is in vain. All hatred is in vain....

With this overcoming of hatred, with this exclusion of it from the inventory of the powers of the soul, the way opens up for the peace of soul. Only now can I achieve repose of my mind; only now can I achieve true and permanent contentment. As long as hatred threatens me, my own or another man's, I cannot hope for peace and for genuine contentment. If the misery of war did not rage about us, then even the specter of war, the mere danger of war, would constitute a contradiction to the peace of the world, as well as to the peace of the soul. We do not have it, no people has it, mankind does not have it, as long as the phantom of hatred among peoples, this actual angel of death, traverses the world with his scythe. Nor can the individual man attain peace of soul without securing the peace of the world. Messianism unites humanity with every individual man. For my own peace I need the confidence that hatred among peoples will be destroyed from the consciousness of mankind. Peoples do not hate one another, but greed awakens envy, and greed and envy delude man with an illusory image, which one passes off as a power of the soul, and which one presumes to confirm as such. All hatred is vain and wanton. All hatred is nothing but illusion, nothing but the interpretation and embellishment of human baseness, which is constituted by greed and selfishness and their effect, envy. If one recognizes the illusion of a false national psychology, which in all peoples is constituted by hatred; if one recognizes in a more fundamental psychology, which is enlightened by ethics, that hatred is an illusory factor in the soul, then the greater part of the burden of sin falls from the human heart. There is no hatred when peace has pitched its tent in the heart of man. "The tent of peace" (*sukkat shalom*) is therefore used in prayer. The tent is the tabernacle that has acquired such a deep symbolic meaning that a holy day has been dedicated to it. The Feast of Tabernacles is the true feast of peace during the wandering through the desert of earthly existence. Peace makes all of life into a feast. Peace brings the peace of nature into the human world, it brings the mood of naiveté into the reflection upon the world. We no longer believe in the experience of history which passes itself off as the wisdom of history, according to which everything has been and always will be the same: individuals and peoples hate each other, and hatred is an instinctual power of human consciousness. We do not trust pessimism; we despise its wisdom, because we have understood the meaning of the world more profoundly and correctly....

Again we have to point to the important saying of the Talmud, that the soul, when it is led before the heavenly judge, has to give an answer to the question: "Did you hope for redemption?" Redemption, however, is world peace. The Jew is to nourish and carry this hope in his heart. It has become an article of faith. Monotheism and Messianism have grown into each other. If world peace is the innermost belief of the religious consciousness, then peace must be an unfailing power, a reliable guide of the mind. In the testimony of religion, peace is the characteristic of the historical world. Therefore peace must also be the power of soul of the individual consciousness. All the disturbances and doubts of peace are impediments to the life of the soul; they are misinterpretations and pathological aberrations. The fundamental power of the human soul is as certainly peace, as peace is the goal of human history.[1]

Primary Sources

INTRODUCTION

Here reconciliation is the reconciliation of the finite of limited and imperfect man with the infinite of the commandment. This reconciliation occurs when our enemy becomes our fellow man, when he returns to himself and the origin and path of his life. Then we can therefore find him and he can find us. Whoever is able to lead him to that point has proven the moral power of love. "That man is a hero," says the Talmud, "who can make a friend out of a foe." For thereby is fulfilled the yearning for the love of fellow man. "When a man's ways please the Lord, he makes even his enemies be at peace with him" (Prov. 16:7). In accordance with this sentence from the Bible, the Talmudic master Rabbi Judah prayed: "O that the sinners may become perfect so that they cease to be evildoers." Rabbi Eleazar prayed: "Grant, O Lord, my God, and God of my fathers, that there should not arise hatred against us in any man's heart, and that there should not arise hatred against any man in our heart." In this desire all hatred has died and the path to peace is before us.[2]   *Leo Baeck*

The Lord bless you and protect you! The Lord deal kindly and graciously with you! The Lord bestow His favor upon you and grant you peace!   *Numbers 6:24–26*

～

You shall not steal; you shall not deal deceitfully or falsely with one another. You shall not swear falsely by My name, profaning the name of your God: I am the Lord.

You shall not defraud your fellow. You shall not commit robbery. The wages of a laborer shall not remain with you until morning.

You shall not insult the deaf, or place a stumbling block before the blind. You shall fear your God: I am the Lord. You shall not render an unfair decision: do not favor the poor or show deference to the rich; judge your kinsman fairly. Do not deal basely with your countrymen. Do not profit by the blood of your fellow: I am the Lord.

Leviticus 19:11–16

⌒

Then the officials shall address the troops, as follows: "Is there anyone who has built a new house but has not dedicated it? Let him go back to his home, lest he die in battle and another dedicate it. Is there anyone who has planted a vineyard but has never harvested it? Let him go back to his home, lest he die in battle and another harvest it. Is there anyone who has paid the bride-price for a wife, but who has not yet married her? Let him go back to his home, lest he die in battle and another marry her."

Deuteronomy 20:5–7

⌒

In the days to come,
The Mount of the Lord's House
Shall stand firm above the mountains
And tower above the hills;
And all the nations
Shall gaze on it with joy.
And the many people shall go and say:
"Come,
Let us go up to the Mount of the Lord,
To the House of the God of Jacob;
That He may instruct us in His ways,
And that we may walk in His paths."
For instruction shall come forth from Zion,
The word of the Lord from Jerusalem.
Thus He will judge among the nations
And arbitrate for the many peoples,

And they shall beat their swords into plowshares
>And their spears into pruning hooks:
>Nation shall not take up
>Sword against nation;
>They shall never again know war.
>O House of Jacob!
>Come, let us walk
>By the light of the Lord.

Isaiah 2:2–5

~

And seek the welfare of the city to which I have exiled you and pray to the Lord in its behalf; for in its prosperity you shall prosper.   *Jeremiah 29:7*

~

Come, my sons, listen to me; I will teach you what it is to fear the Lord. Who is the man who is eager for life, who desires years of good fortune? Guard your tongue from evil, your lips from deceitful speech. Shun evil and do good, seek amity and pursue it.

Psalm 34:12–15

~

Then he summoned his son Solomon and charged him with building the House for the Lord God of Israel. David said to Solomon, "My son, I wanted to build a House for the name of the Lord my God. But the word of the Lord came to me, saying, 'You have shed much blood and fought great battles; you shall not build a House for My name for you have shed much blood on the earth in My sight. But you will have a son who will be a man at rest, for I will give him rest from all his enemies on all sides; Solomon will be his name and I shall confer peace and quiet on Israel in his time.'"

I Chronicles 22:6–9

~

There are other charitable and very merciful regulations as to the treatment of enemies in wartime. They must not he declares be yet regarded as enemies, even if they [Israel] are at the gates or stationed beside the walls in full array and planting their engines, until envoys have been sent with invitations to peace.[3]

Philo of Alexandria

⌇

The duty of sharing with others was inculcated by our legislator in other matters. We must furnish fire, water, food to all who ask for them, point out the road, not leave a corpse unburied, show consideration even to declared enemies. He does not allow us to burn up their country or to cut down their fruit trees, and forbids even the spoiling of fallen combatants; he has taken measures to prevent outrage to prisoners of war, especially women.[4]

Flavius Josephus

⌇

R. Pedas said in the name of R. Yaakov bar Idi: R. Elazar would pray additional prayers after he would conclude each of his three daily *Shemoneh Esrei* prayers. What additional prayers would he say? May it be Your will, *Hashem*, my God and the God of my fathers, that hatred of us not enter the heart of any man and that hatred of no man enter our hearts, that jealousy of us not enter the heart of any man and that jealousy of any man not enter our hearts. And may Your Torah be our occupation for all of our lives; and may our words be proper entreaties before You.[5]

Jerusalem Talmud, Berakhot 4:2

⌇

There were once some highwaymen in the neighborhood of R. Meir who caused him a great deal of trouble. R. Meir accordingly prayed that they should die. His wife Beruria said to him: How do you make out [that such a prayer should be permitted]? Because it is written Let *hatta'im* [sin] cease? Is it written *hot'im* [sinner]? It is written *hatta'im*! Further, look at the end of the verse: *and let the wicked men be no more*. Since the sins will cease, there will be no more wicked men! Rather pray for them that they should repent, and there will be no more wicked. He did pray for them, and they repented.   *Babylonian Talmud*, Berakhot 10a

A favorite saying of Abaye was: A man should always be subtle in the fear of heaven. *A soft answer turneth away wrath*, and one should always strive to be on the best terms with his brethren and his relatives and with all men and even with the heathen in the street, in order that he may be beloved above and well-liked below and be acceptable to his fellow creatures. It was related of R. Johanan b. Zakkai that no man ever gave him greeting first, even a heathen in the street.   *Babylonian Talmud*, Berakhot 17a

R. Beroka Hoza'ah used to frequent the market at Be Lapat where Elijah often appeared to him. Once he asked [the prophet], Is there anyone in this market who has a share in the world to come? He replied, No.... Whilst [they were thus conversing] two [men] passed by and [Elijah] remarked, These two have a share in the world to come. R. Beroka then approached and asked them, What is your occupation? They replied, We are Jesters, when we see men depressed we cheer them up; furthermore when we see two people quarrelling we strive hard to make peace between them.
                    Babylonian Talmud, Taanit 22a

R. Ile'a further stated in the name of R. Eleazar son of R. Simeon: One may modify a statement in the interests of peace; for it is said in Scripture, *Thy father did command ... so shall ye say unto Joseph: Forgive....*   *Babylonian Talmud*, Yevamot 65b

And there went out the song throughout the host: R. Aha b. Hanina said: [It is the song referred to in the verse,] *When the wicked perish, there is song;* [thus] when Ahab b. Omri perished there was "song." But does the Holy One, blessed be He, rejoice over the downfall of the wicked? Is it not written, [*That they should praise*] *as they went out before the army, and say, Give thanks unto the Lord for His mercy endureth for ever;* concerning which R. Jonathan asked: Why are the words, *He is good,* omitted from this expression of thanks? Because the Holy One, blessed be He, does not rejoice in the downfall of the wicked. For R. Samuel b. Nahman said in R. Jonathan's name: What is meant by, *And one approached not the other all night?* In that hour the ministering angels wished to utter the song [of praise] before the Holy One, blessed be He, but He rebuked them, saying: My handiwork [the Egyptians] is drowning in the sea; would ye utter song before me!

Babylonian Talmud, Sanhedrin 39b

~

Hillel said, "Be one of Aaron's students, loving peace and pursuing it, loving people and bringing them to the Torah."

Pirke Avot/Sayings of the Fathers 1:12

Now the Torah did not insist that we should actually go in pursuit of the commandments.... In the case of peace, however, *"seek peace"* wherever you happen to be, *"and pursue it"* if it is elsewhere.[6]   *Midrash Numbers Rabbah (on Numbers 19:27)*

~

God told Moses to fight against Sihon and Og, as it is written: ENGAGE THEM IN WAR. But he did not do so. Rather he sent emissaries of peace to Sihon, the king of Heshbon. The Holy One of Blessing declared: I told you to fight them, but you tried to make peace. By your life, I make a decree that each war shall first be preceded by attempts at peace, as it is written: When you approach a city (to make war)....[7]   *Midrash Deuteronomy Rabbah 5:12*

Resh Lakish said: Great is peace, for Scripture gave fictitious reasons in order to make peace between Joseph and his brethren. When their father died, they feared lest he would avenge himself on them. And what did they say to him? *Thy father did command before he died, saying: So shall ye say unto Joseph* (Gen. 50:16f). And yet nowhere do we find that Jacob our father had so commanded. Scripture, however, made use of fictitious reasons in the interests of peace.[8]

Midrash Deuteronomy Rabbah 5:15

When the Holy One, blessed be He, created the first man, He took him and led him round all the trees of the Garden of Eden, and said to him, "Behold My works, how beautiful and commendable they are! All that I have created, for your sake I created it. Pay heed that you do not corrupt and destroy My universe; for if you corrupt it there is no one to repair it after you."[9]

Midrash Ecclesiastes Rabbah 7:13

"And the Land shall yield her produce" (Lev. 26:4). You might say, "Well, we've got food, we've got drink." Still, if there is no peace, there is nothing at all, for Scripture goes on to say, "And I will give peace in the Land" (Ps. 26:6), which indicates that peace equals all else. Indeed, we say [in the morning *Tefillah*], "When He made peace, He created everything."

R. Levi said: Peace is precious, for the blessings [following the Shema and the blessing at the end of the *Tefillah*] conclude with peace. Then, too, the priests' blessing ends with "The Lord give thee peace" (Num. 6:26), by way of saying that none of the blessings avail at all unless peace is with them.

R. Eleazar ha-Kappar said: Great is peace, for even when Israel worship idols but are together in one band, the measure of justice does not touch them, as it is said, "Ephraim is banded to idols, let him alone" (Hos. 4:17). But when they are divided, what is said of them? "Their heart is divided—let them now bear their guilt" (Hos. 10:2).

Hezekiah said: Great is peace, for Scripture says of all the other journeys, "They journeyed" and "They encamped," that is to say, they set out in strife and encamped in strife. But when they came to Sinai, they encamped as a single encampment: "Israel, there he encamped before the mount" (Exod. 19:2). Then the Holy One said: Since they have learned to hate strife and love peace, so that they are now encamped as a single encampment, the time has come for Me to give them My Torah.

R. Eliezer said: Great is peace, for the prophets have implanted in the mouths of people nought but peace.

Bar Kappara said: Great is peace, for even those on high require peace, as it is said, "He maketh peace among those of His on high" (Job 25:2). Now, the matter may be argued a fortiori: if those on high—among whom there is no hatred, no enmity, no jealousy, no rivalry, no grudging eye—require peace, all the more and more so do human beings, among whom there are such [evil] traits.

R. Joshua said: Great is peace, for the Holy One Himself is called Peace, as it is said, "And he called it the 'Lord is peace'" (Judg. 6:24).

R. Joshua ben Levi said: Great is peace; peace is to the world as leaven is to dough.

Great is peace, for even the dead require peace, as when God said to Abram, "Thou shalt go to thy fathers in peace" (Gen. 15:15).

R. Ishmael said: Great is peace, for we find that the Holy One allowed His Name, which is written [in the Torah] in sanctity, to be erased by water in order to bring peace between husband and wife.

Great is peace. For the sake of peace, the Holy One changed words a person uttered, as when the angel quoted Sarah as having said, "Shall I of a surety bear a child, who am old?" (Gen. 18:13).[10]

Aggadic tradition

It is grounded in our reason that the shedding of human blood cannot be allowed, so that one does not destroy the other and by adding to severe sorrow thwart the notion that the All-Wise had with creation; for murder would do away with the purpose for which he has made human beings and graced them with knowledge.[11]   *Saadya Fayyumi (Saadya Gaon)*

Let no one think that in the days of the Messiah any of the laws of nature will be set aside, or any innovation be introduced into creation. The world will follow its normal course. The words of Isaiah: *And the wolf shall dwell with the lamb, and the leopard shall lie down with the kid* (Isa. 11:6) are to be understood figuratively, meaning that Israel will live securely among the wicked of the heathen who are likened to wolves and leopards, as it is written: A wolf of the deserts doth spoil them, a leopard watcheth over their cities (Jer. 5:6).... All similar expressions used in connection with the Messianic age are metaphorical....

Said the Rabbis: *The sole difference between the present and the Messianic days is delivery from servitude to foreign powers* (B. San. 91b)....

The sages and Prophets did not long for the days of the Messiah that Israel might exercise dominion over the world, or rule over the heathens, or be exalted by the nations, or that it might eat and drink and rejoice. Their aspiration was that Israel be free to devote itself to the Law and its wisdom, with no one to oppress or disturb it, and thus be worthy of life in the world to come.

In that era there will be neither famine nor war, neither jealousy nor strife. Blessings will be abundant, comforts within the reach of all. The one preoccupation of the whole world will be to know the Lord.[12]   *Moses Maimonides*

Before beginning one's prayers, one should concentrate on the thought of loving one's fellow creatures.[13]

Isaac Ben Solomon Luria (Ha-Ari)

∽

Our wise men teach: "Seek peace in your place!" Only he who seeks peace nowhere other than in himself will find it.[14]

Baal Shem Tov

∽

But in man himself, even in his body, you must respect the Divine spirit which God has breathed into him so that he may in emulation of God dispose of his body and life on earth according to God's will. You must not deprive this Divine spirit in man of its bodily frame; the body belongs to this spirit, just as it in turn belongs to God. You must not sever the tie by which God has tied the body to the Divine spirit in man to the human soul. You must not kill![15]

Samson Raphael Hirsch

∽

That it is altogether in the spirit of Rabbinical teaching to consider the association of souls itself as the highest requirement of morality, appears from its wellnigh inexhaustible treatment of the idea of peace. No chapter of the doctrine of morality is developed with such exuberance of thought and depth of feeling as that on the value of peace among men. No less an authority than Rabbi himself is reported to have said: "If the Israelites were to practise idolatry"—one of the three capital crimes always grouped together—"but peace prevailed among them at the same time, God would say, as it were, 'I cannot exercise my angry authority against them, because peace is among them.'" They enjoy immunity, so to speak, on account of the one ideal which they realize.[16]

Moritz Lazarus

∽

One of the most significant sections of our ancient law is the distinction between an ordinary war against a "very distant" people, conducted according to the general rules of the laws of war which regard war as an ordinary expression of the life of comparable states, and the holy war against the "seven nations" of Canaan, by means of which God's people conquers the area necessary for its existence. This distinction contains within it a new view of war as an action necessary for God's sake. The peoples of the Christian Era can no longer maintain this distinction. In keeping with the spirit of Christianity, which admits of no boundaries, there are for it no "very distant" peoples. Holy war and political war, which in Jewish law were constitutionally distinguished, are here blended into one....

As against the life of the nations of the world, constantly involved in a holy war, the Jewish people has left its holy war behind in its mythical antiquity. Hence, whatever wars it experiences are purely political wars. But since the concept of a holy war is ingrained in it, it cannot take these wars as seriously as the peoples of antiquity to whom such a concept was alien. In the whole Christian world, the Jew is practically the only human being who cannot take war seriously, and this makes him the only genuine pacifist.[17]   *Franz Rosenzweig*

~

May the spirit of brotherly love and mutual understanding heal all wounds. O Lord, let the tumult of war fall silent to the ends of the earth, so that each can sit by his vine and under his fig tree and no one make him afraid: ... Grant, O heavenly Father, that your kingdom, the kingdom of truth and peace, may extend, and bring near the days when you are acknowledged as Lord of the whole earth. Amen![18]   *From the Jewish liturgy*

Core Ethic 4

Justice: commitment to a
culture of justice and a just
economic order.

Public Prosperity

Salomo Samuel

As far as we can see, the ancient Jewish state for the first time elevated social welfare for the economically weak and in order to fight human distress from the chance occurrences of personal help and made it an urgent and comprehensive public task. The principle (Lev. 25:35) "If your brother wavers beside you and his hand become slack, protect him, even the stranger and sojourner, *so that he lives alongside you*" is matched by measures of such a unique character that they resist any attempt to demonstrate alien derivation. We mention the treatment of servants and slaves; the Sabbath, the fallow year and the year of Jubilee; the regulations for harvest, conditions for debt and pledging. All initially presupposed that the people were settled in the holy land; how perfectly they must have corresponded to the public spirit and by being practiced became completely fused with it, since when the Jewish form of the state was shattered they immediately became crystallized in new forms.

In the state we encounter *ebed ibri*, the serving Hebrew, whom we must take care not to call slave, because he lacks essential marks of slavery. Strictly speaking he has always put himself (*nimkar*) in the relationship of service voluntarily and for a period; his labor has been acquired (*nikna*) for a time; he retains his innate human dignity and human rights. Only by incurring debt could the free man be handed over to the injured party by the court; violent imposition of slavery for debt was regarded a grave injustice and fought against. The one who sold himself to the stranger (sojourner) in economic need put an obligation on all his relations with possessions to redeem him. Differing from the hireling only by the more fixed period of time in respect of his "double contribution" (Deut.15:18), he is not released to build up a new economic independence without the offering of rich gifts. The non-Jew bought abroad was a slave in the narrower sense. But in contrast to the Codex Hammurabi (§§117–119, cf. §§278–282), the inhabitant of the land who had been pledged (i.e. who was in service) for a time encountered only protective measures, whereas the slave was treated as a thing; the old Jewish law also knows a right of the slave. He too may not be put under harsh pressure; gross maltreatment results in his liberation; in the rabbinic view he is also free in the year of Jubilee (see below). Thus in Israel there were no slave revolts; even the threat of broad strata of the population for heavy indebtedness was easily overcome, at least after the exile; one might compare the ignominious behavior of the people in the time of Jeremiah (34.8ff.) with the generous resolution in the time of Nehemiah (ch. 5).

The agricultural regulations form a network of well-organized social welfare. Here the basic notion is that God alone is the proprietor of the soil of the holy land; the children of Israel are strangers or sojourners with him; their leasing contract with God obligates them to far-reaching concern for those who are protected by God, the economically weak. There was the Sabbath, which guarantees the servant and the maidservant a full day of rest; the seventh year, the so-called Shemitta, and the fiftieth, i.e., the year of Jubilee with its impositions for those with possessions and its relief for those without. There was the urgent question whether the limits of the attainable had not been exceeded and the implementation of a fallow or Jubilee year was not utterly utopian. The history of the second state at least teaches us that this was taken very seriously. The favors which the poor enjoyed at every harvest existed from time immemorial: the gleanings, what had been forgotten, the corners of the field (*leket, schikcha, pea*); there was also the tithe (*maaser*) in its various forms. Thus a proletariat could not form in ancient Israel, and the biblical writings have no expression for beggar.

These measures were completed by regulations about the lending of money and goods and about pledges, which worked in the same direction. Like speedy recompense for the hireling and craftsman, they all made no distinction between Jews and non-Jews; only lending without usury with complete remission in the seventh year was understandably limited to members of the people.

Long before the destruction of the Second Temple the countless communities outside the holy land had taken fire from the fire of the altar everywhere and guarded it. The altar of brotherly love was very appropriate, around which formerly the communities of the dispersion formed themselves as around prayer and scholarship. The contribution made by these communities to public prosperity in the sphere of social ethics from then on, in their sphere after the loss of land and state, army and hierarchy of officials, was amazing; it was the model for the earliest Christian communities. In keeping with the changed conditions new institutions formed alongside old ones, new names alongside old ones: *tamhuy*, feeding the people; *kuppa*, cash box for the poor; *chebrot* (associations) for special purposes, for example endowing poor brides, the care of the sick and funerals; an authentic Jewish need, the need of a community, whose members were cruelly flung around in the world, directed the *pidyon shewuyim* (cash box) which the captive fellow-Jew had to administer (especially in ports). The tasks which the community expected its members to perform for the numerous branches of public prosperity were great, sometimes oppressive; but the administration of these sums collected under the name of *hekdesh* money was precisely prescribed in voluntary terms. To this was added the oath-money (*nedarim*), voluntary, but also public because it was given in the sight of the community with an appeal to the Torah, almost always for charitable purposes.

In support of the predominant principle of "supporting and strengthening the wavering brother" it was already possible through timely intervention to avoid total collapse, to prefer lending to alms, to provide greater means for bringing independence without interest. It is superfluous to emphasize that there had to be careful consideration, so that benevolence did not get above itself; perhaps it is not superfluous to say that the heart should dominate. The needs of daily life, the degree of need, the mental constitution of the one seeking help (whether man or woman, and so on), all this was weighed up with head and heart. The obligation to contribute was fixed according to the duration of residence and the economic situation; in the case of human needs no distinction was made between Jews and non-Jews in need of help, because peaceful agreement should prevail in society. A deeply religious notion still today dominates the whole sphere of the Jewish cultivation of welfare: "Whoever accepts the poor as it were reconciles himself with his creator."[1]

Primary Sources

INTRODUCTION

The beginning of the social in Judaism is the recognition of one man by another. The human right here is above all the right of the fellow human being, the life on which he has a claim alongside us. "Your brother shall live with you." The very words "your brother" here contain everything; it is the core from which everything else grows. Man and fellow-man here belong together. The other is the same as me; he is in all essentials and peculiarities like me, he is being of my being; the dignity which makes me a human being is also his human dignity. "You shall love your neighbor as yourself...."

A circle may not be separated off by benevolence and inclination, but every human being, including the stranger and the one of another kind, even the one who is or was or still is our enemy, has a claim on us. Everyone is our brother and our neighbor and therefore has the right to us, the right of his humanity to our fellow-humanity. What we do to him is therefore not something else, something extraordinary, but is *tzedakah*, righteousness, the simple commandment that can be taken for granted. The social represents positive righteousness alongside merely negative, legalistic righteousness.

By it the moral community is created, the state in its positive, social sense, the society of those who belong together by custom, the state of the *tzedakah*. Human tasks and human works now bring together that which the shared natural or historical ground supports. Anyone who wants to stand alone, to work and toil only for himself, has already done an injustice to this community, to this state, even if he is blameless in a negatively bourgeois sense. It is the fulfillment of social obligations that makes him a citizen here; the state is a state of fellow human beings....

Love of neighbor belongs to the social sphere, as longing and feeling belong to the human sphere, to humanity. We should also take part inwardly in the feelings of our fellow human being, understand the longing of his disposition, the weal and woe of his heart. Not only the heart but the soul should also be alive in the social dimension. The community should be a community of those who are inwardly bound together, a community of peace.

The social idea then found its last and supreme expression in the Jewish, messianic notion of the kingdom of God. All human beings are to come together in this social sphere, create the humanity of the *tzedakah*. There are limits set by power, limits which are established by utility; there are no state limits, no advantageous limits to the commandment, the social obligation. The decision for one's fellow human being sees what is near everywhere, always sees the neighbor, the human brother. All that is human is on the horizon here. The lands and the days are united in the commandment. Human beings become humanity in the social idea.[2]   *Leo Baeck*

If you take your neighbor's garment in pledge, you must return it to him before the sun sets; it is his only clothing, the sole covering for his skin. In what else shall he sleep? Therefore, if he cries out to Me, I will pay heed, for I am compassionate.

Exodus 22:25–26

When you reap the harvest of your land, you shall not reap all the way to the edges of your field, or gather the gleanings of your harvest. You shall not pick your vineyard bare, or gather the fallen fruit of your vineyard; you shall leave them for the poor and the stranger: I the Lord am your God.

Leviticus 19:9–10

You shall not abuse a needy and destitute laborer, whether a fellow countryman or a stranger in one of the communities of your land.   *Deuteronomy 24:14*

You shall not subvert the rights of the stranger or the fatherless;
you shall not take a widow's garment in pawn.

Deuteronomy 24:17

Learn to do good.
Devote yourselves to justice;
Aid the wronged.
Uphold the rights of the orphan;
Defend the cause of the widow.

Isaiah 1:17

He who walks in righteousness,
Speaks uprightly,
Spurns profit from fraudulent dealings,
Waves away a bribe instead of grasping it,
Stops his ears against listening to infamy,
Shuts his eyes against looking at evil—
Such a one shall dwell in lofty security,
With inaccessible cliffs for his stronghold,
With his food supplied
And his drink assured.

Isaiah 33:15–16

No, this is the fast I desire:
To unlock fetters of wickedness,
And untie the cords of the yoke
To let the oppressed go free;
To break off every yoke.
It is to share your bread with the hungry,
And to take the wretched poor into your home;

When you see the naked, to clothe him,
And not to ignore your own kin.

Isaiah 58:6–7

∽

Thus said the Lord: Do what is just and right; rescue from the defrauder him who is robbed; do not wrong the stranger, the fatherless, and the widow; commit no lawless act, and do not shed the blood of the innocent in this place.

Jeremiah 22:3

∽

He has told you, O man, what is good,
And what the Lord requires of you:
Only to do justice
And to love goodness,
And to walk modestly with your God.

Micah 6:8

∽

They say, "By our tongues we shall prevail;
with lips such as ours, who can be our master?
Because of the groans of the plundered poor and needy,
I will now act," says the Lord.
"I will give help," He affirms to him.

Psalm 12:5–6

∽

The righteous bloom like a date-palm;
they thrive like a cedar in Lebanon.

Psalm 92:13

∽

Be as a father to orphans, and in place of a husband to widows; then God will call thee "son," and will be gracious to thee, and deliver thee from the Pit.   *Ben Sirakh 4:10*

⸺

Keep, therefore, my children, the law of God, and get singleness, and walk in guilelessness, not playing the busybody with your neighbor, but love the Lord and your neighbor, have compassion on the poor and weak.

Testaments of the Twelve Patriarchs 5:5

⸺

But among the vast number of particular truths and principles here studied, there stand out practically high above the others two main heads: one of duty to God as shewn by piety and holiness, one of duty to men as shewn by humanity and justice.[3]

Philo of Alexandria

⸺

Nor yet, when autumn fruits are at their prime, must ye forbid wayfarers to touch them, but let them take their fill, as if they were their own, be they natives or strangers, rejoicing at thus affording them a share in the fruits of the season.... Neither let the vintagers hinder such as they meet from eating of that which they are carrying to the wine-vats; for it were unjust to grudge the good things which by God's will have come into the world to such as long for a share in them, when the season is at its prime and so swiftly to pass. Nay, it would be acceptable to God that one should even invite to take thereof any who, through modesty, should hesitate to touch them—be they Israelites, as partners and owners, in virtue of their kinship, be they come from another country, entreating them to accept, as guests, of these gifts which God has granted them in season.[4]

Flavius Josephus

~

Our Rabbis taught: Formerly they were wont to convey [victuals] to the house of mourning, the rich in silver and gold baskets and the poor in osier baskets of peeled willow twigs, and the poor felt shamed: they therefore instituted that all should convey [victuals] in osier baskets of peeled willow twigs out of deference to the poor. Our Rabbis taught: Formerly, they were wont to serve drinks in a house of mourning, the rich in white glass vessels and the poor in colored glass, and the poor felt shamed: they instituted therefore that all should serve drinks in colored glass, out of deference to the poor. Formerly they were wont to uncover the face of the rich and cover the face of the poor, because their faces turned livid in years of drought and the poor felt shamed: they therefore instituted that everybody's face should be covered, out of deference for the poor. Formerly, they were wont to bring out the rich [for burial] on a dargesh and the poor on a plain bier, and the poor felt shamed: they instituted therefore that all should be brought out on a plain bier, out of deference for the poor.

Babylonian Talmud, Mo'ed Katan 27a–27b

~

R. Simlai when preaching said: Six hundred and thirteen precepts were communicated to Moses, three hundred and sixty-five negative precepts, corresponding to the number of solar days [in the year], and two hundred and forty-eight positive precepts, corresponding to the number of the members of man's body. Said R. Hamnuna: What is the [authentic] text for this? It is, *Moses commanded us torah, an inheritance of the congregation of Jacob*, 'torah' being in letter-value equal to six hundred and eleven, '*I am*' and '*Thou shalt have no* [*other Gods*]' [not being reckoned, because] we heard from the mouth of the Mighty [Divine]. David came and reduced them to eleven [principles], as it is written, *A Psalm of David. Lord, who shall sojourn in Thy tabernacle? Who shall dwell in Thy holy mountain?*—[i] *He that walketh uprightly, and* [ii] *wor-*

keth righteousness, and [iii] speaketh truth in his heart; that [iv] hath no slander upon his tongue, [v] nor doeth evil to his fellow, [vi] nor taketh up a reproach against his neighbor, [vii] in whose eyes a vile person is despised, but [viii] he honoreth them that fear the Lord, [ix] He sweareth to his own hurt and changeth not, [x] He putteth not out his money on interest, [xi] nor taketh a bribe against the innocent. He that doeth these things shall never be moved. "He that walketh uprightly": that was Abraham, as it is written, *Walk before Me and be thou whole-hearted.* "And worketh righteousness," such as Abba Hilkiahu. "Speaketh truth in his heart," such as R. Safra. "Hath no slander upon his tongue," that was our Father Jacob, as it is written, *My father peradventure will feel me and I shall seem to him as a deceiver.* "Nor doeth evil to his fellow," that is he who does not set up in opposition to his fellow craftsman. *"Nor taketh up a reproach against his neighbor,"* that is he who befriends his near ones [relatives]. *"In whose eyes a vile person is despised,"* that was Hezekiah the king [of Judah] who dragged his father's bones on a rope truckle-bed. *"He honoreth them that fear the Lord,"* that was Jehoshaphat king of Judah, who every time he beheld a scholar–disciple rose from his throne, and embraced and kissed him, calling him Father, Father; Rabbi, Rabbi; Mari Mari! *"He sweareth to his own hurt and changeth not,"* like R. Johanan; for R. Johanan [once] said: I shall remain fasting until I reach home. *"He putteth not out money on interest"* not even interest from a heathen. *"Nor taketh a bribe against the innocent,"* such as R. Ishmael son of R. Jose. It is written [in conclusion], *He that doeth these things shall never be moved.* Whenever R. Gamaliel came to this passage he used to weep, saying: [Only] one who practiced all these shall not be moved; but anyone falling short in any of these [virtues] would be moved! Said his colleagues to him: Is it written, "He that doeth all these things [shall not fall]"? It reads, *"He that doeth these things,"* meaning even if only he practices one of these things [he shall not be moved]. For if you say otherwise, what of that other [similar] passage, *Defile not ye yourselves in all these things?* Are we to say that one who seeks contact with all these vices, he is become contaminated; but if only with one of those vices, he is not contaminated? [Surely,] it can only mean there, that if he seeks contact with any one of these vices he is become contaminated, and likewise here, if he practises even one of these virtues [he will not be moved].

Isaiah came and reduced them to six [principles], as it is written, [i] *He that walketh righteously, and* [ii] *speaketh uprightly,* [iii] *He that despiseth the gain of oppressions,* [iv] *that shaketh his hand from holding of bribes,* [v] *that stoppeth his ear from hearing of blood,* [vi] *and shutteth his eyes from looking upon evil; he shall dwell on high.* "*He that walketh righteously,*" that was our Father Abraham, as it is written, *For I have known him, to the end that he may command his children and his household after him,* etc.; "*and speaketh uprightly,*" that is one who does not put an affront on his fellow in public. "*He that despiseth the gain of oppressions,*" as, for instance, R. Ishmael b. Elisha; "*that shaketh his hand from holding of bribes,*" as, for instance, R. Ishmael son of Jose; "*that stoppeth his ear from hearing of blood,*" one who hears not aspersions made against a rabbinic student and remains silent, as once did R. Eleazar son of R. Simeon; "*and shutteth his eyes from looking upon evil*" as R. Hiyya b. Abba [taught]; for R. Hiyya b. Abba said: This refers to one who does not peer at women as they stand washing clothes [in the court-yard] and [concerning such a man] it is written, *He shall dwell on high.*

Micah came and reduced them to three [principles], as it is written, *It hath been told thee, O man, what is good, and what the Lord doth require of thee:* [i] *only to do justly, and* [ii] *to love mercy and* [iii] *to walk humbly before thy God.* "*To do justly,*" that is, maintaining justice; "*and to love mercy,*" that is, rendering every kind office; "*and walking humbly before thy God,*" that is, walking in funeral and bridal processions. And do not these facts warrant an *a fortiori* conclusion, that if in matters that are not generally performed in private the Torah enjoins "walking humbly," is it not ever so much more requisite in matters that usually call for modesty?

Again came Isaiah and reduced them to two [principles], as it is said, *Thus saith the Lord, [i] Keep ye justice and [ii] do righteousness* [etc.]. Amos came and reduced them to one [principle], as it is said, *For thus saith the Lord unto the house of Israel, Seek ye Me and live.* To this R. Nahman b. Isaac demurred, saying: [Might it not be taken as,] Seek Me by observing the whole Torah and live? But it is Habakkuk who came and based them all on one [principle], as it is said, *But the righteous shall live by his faith.*
Babylonian Talmud, Makkot 23b–24a

There are four kinds of people who would give to charity. One wishes to give but [believes] that others should not. That one's eye is evil to those others. One [wishes that] others give and that he should not. His eye is evil toward himself. One [wishes that] he should give and so should others. That one is a saint. [The] one [who believes that he] should not give nor should others is a sinner.
Pirke Avot/Sayings of the Fathers 5:13

The Lord loveth the righteous (Ps. 146:8).... And why does God love the righteous? Because their righteousness is not something inherited, as is the priesthood in a family of priests or in a family of Levites.... But should a man seek to become righteous, even if he is a gentile, he can become righteous; for the righteous do not depend upon a family line, but in their own persons volunteer and come to love the Holy One, blessed be He, as it is said, *Rejoice in the Lord, O ye righteous* (Ps. 33:1). Hence it is said, *The Lord loveth the righteous.*[5]
Midrash Tehillim (to Ps. 146:8)

I bear witness by heaven and earth: be a person Jewish or non-Jewish, man or woman, slave or free—the spirit of God rests on all human beings solely according to the measure of their good works.[6]
Seder Eliyahu Rabbah

⁓

Let a man do good works and then seek God's instruction. Let a man do just and good works and then seek God's wisdom. Let a man choose the way of humility and then seek God's understanding.[7]

Seder Eliyahu Rabbah

⁓

There are eight degrees of almsgiving, each one superior to the other. The highest degree, than which there is none higher, is one who upholds the hand of an Israelite reduced to poverty by handing him a gift or a loan, or entering into a partnership with him, or finding work for him, in order to strengthen his hand, so that he would have no need to beg from other people.... Below this is he who gives alms to the poor in such a way that he does not know to whom he has given, nor does the poor man know from whom he has received.... Below this is he who knows to whom he is giving, while the poor man does not know from whom he is receiving.... Below this is the case where the poor man knows from whom he is receiving, but himself remains unknown to the giver. Below this is he who hands the alms to the poor man before being asked for them. Below this is he who hands the alms to the poor man after the latter has asked for them. Below this is he who gives the poor man less than what is proper, but with a friendly countenance. Below this is he who gives alms with a frowning countenance.[8]

Moses Maimonides

⁓

Consider the trait of cleanness in relation to deceit. How we are liable to yield to the temptation of acting deceitfully! For example, it is evidently proper for a man to praise his wares, or, by resorting to persuasion, to earn for his labor as much as he can. We say of such a man that he is ambitious and will succeed (Pes. 50b).... But, unless he is very careful to weigh his actions, the outcome is bound to be evil instead of good. He will sin and act dishonestly in violation of the precept, "Ye shall not wrong one another" (Lev. 25:17). Our Sages said, "It is forbidden to deceive even a non-Jew" (Hul. 94a).... They said further, "One who despoils his neighbor, even of a farthing's worth, is as though he had deprived him of his life" (B. K. 119a).... "When the sins are gathered into a heap, the sin of robbery is placed on top" (Lev. R. 33:3).... It is perfectly proper to point out to the buyer any good quality which the thing for sale really possess. Fraud consists in hiding the defects in one's wares and is forbidden. This is an important principle in the matter of business honesty.[9]

Moses Hayyim Luzzatto

Be concerned about your own soul and your neighbor's body, not about your own body and another's soul.[10]

Menachem Mendel of Kozk

We must take extreme care not to deceive one another. If anyone deceives his neighbor, whether a seller deceives the buyer, or a buyer deceives the seller, he transgresses a prohibitory law. For it is written (Lev. 25:14): "And if thou sell ought to thy neighbor, or buy of thy neighbor's hand, ye shall not wrong one another." According to our Sages (*Shabbat* 31a), this is the first question that a man is asked when brought before the Heavenly Court: "Hast thou been dealing honestly?"[11]

Kitzur Shulchan Arukh 62:1

According to the halachic precept doing good, this ethical obligation inherited from the fathers, should not merely be practiced by those who are richly endowed; everyone without exception is obliged to support anyone in need according to the measure of his possessions. The Jew is obliged to give help to all men and women without distinction.[12]

Moses Bloch

⌒

Justice is the principle of juridical institutes that are the corner-stone of the Noachide legislation: "Judge justly between a man and his fellow" (Deut. 1:16). The prophets complain about nothing more than about false courts of justice. Therefore they make God the advocate of the stranger, the orphan, and the widow....

The principle of justice had as its consequence the relativity of the principle of property—this bulwark of egotism, of eudaemonism, of opportunism and everything else that is opposed to religious morality. It brought forth the law of the Sabbath along with its symbolic extension of the number seven to the fields, to the Year of Release from debts, the Year of Jubilee for landowner-ship, as well as to all other privileges of property with regard to the harvest and the second growth. The religious significance of this social legislation was fortified by the proclamation of the Year of Jubilee on the Day of Atonement. Hence, the atonement became a sign of social freedom....

The Sabbath is not only for the sake of man, as is said in the Talmud (*Mechilta*) and the Gospel (Mark 2:27), but above all for the sake of the slave, for the sake of the worker. This Sabbath sig-nifies at the same time the completion of God's creation of the world. It is the embodiment of all commandments. And all com-mandments and all festive celebrations are a sign of "remembrance of the Exodus from Egypt." Hence, the entire Torah is a remem-brance of the liberation from Egyptian slavery, which, as the cra-dle of the Jewish people, is not deplored, let alone condemned, but celebrated in gratitude.[13]   *Hermann Cohen*

⌒

Poverty is the universal suffering of the human race. Pity must meet poverty if man is finally to arise as an I. Before this social fact of human suffering the primeval human feeling of pity has to flame up; otherwise one would have to despair about human feel-ing in general....

The distinction between religion and mythology, between monotheism and polytheism, again clearly asserts itself here. Polytheism has its center of gravity in the myth. The spell of myth fills the spirit of primitive man much more strongly than his heart can be stirred by suffering and therefore be moved to pity. Tragedy, too, which grows out of myth, is and basically remains a product of polytheism.

Perhaps the absence of tragedy in Israel's mind can be explained through the onesidedness of its monotheism. Suffering is to be resolved in reality and not merely in the illusory feeling of the spectator. The prophet becomes the practical moralist, the politician and jurist, because he intends to end the suffering of the poor. And it is not enough for him to assume these various callings; he has to become a psychologist as well: he must make pity the primeval feeling of man; he must, as it were, discover in pity man as fellowman and *man* in general.[14]

Hermann Cohen

~

The prophet always feels himself to be the advocate of the poor, not because the poor enjoy God's favor by virtue of being poor but because only they need a defender. The rich are reproached not for their wealth but for the unscrupulous way in which many have acquired it. We hear harsh words against the luxury and dissipation that are evident among the prosperous. But this censure is never born of the fury of the enemy of culture who is turned away from the world, to whom wealth and the enjoyment of life are sin, but from indignation at the squandering of things of value the circumspect and right use of which could have relieved many needs. Nowhere does the dismissive condemnation of "temporal goods" betray itself, which can only venture into the light where "this life" is regarded more or less as merely a preparation for a future true life.[15]

Max Wiener

~

From the earliest time the Torah's demand was directed toward the equality of all members of the people, to a complete equality that rests not merely on the written law but is rooted in the moral view of all the parts. The prophets always emphasized this social teaching to the utmost degree; the doctrine of the brotherliness and equal worth of all members of the people takes up a great deal of space in their demands, which were aimed at the moral elevation of the people. It is the foundation of all social morality, which cannot be thought of at all if one class is given privileges and the other is oppressed. Members of other tribes and peoples who have constantly been in the land and put themselves under the protection of the divine laws, even if they did not follow the ritual ceremonies, are also to be like one's fellows. The dominance of the law, under which all stood equally without distinction of rank and even membership of the people rested on *respect for human dignity*, which Judaism first taught. All human beings are equal before God, since they are all created in his image; therefore the state society too cannot tolerate a violation of this dignity in any person.[16]   *Simon Bernfeld*

~

"Ye shall have one manner of law" (Lev. 24:22), meaning not only that the same due processes of law are required in civil as in criminal matters (*Mishnah Sanhedrin* 4:1; *Sifra, Emor* 20:9), but also laying down the general rule that all law must be the same for all (BT *Ketuvot* 33a, BT *Sanhedrin* 28a, BT *Bava Kamma* 83b–84a). This rule is reiterated with special emphasis on the stranger: "One law and one manner shall be for you and for the stranger that sojourneth with you" (Num. 15:16). The force and the protection of the law both extend to everybody, citizen and stranger, man and woman, freeborn and slave, alike. It is true that Talmudical law restricted the binding force of legal obligations to Jews only and held non-Jews bound to obey solely the seven Noachide commands; but the protection of the laws was always extended to non-Jews who chose to avail themselves of it. Thus, Jewish courts will entertain suits of non-Jews who voluntarily submit to their jurisdiction (Maimonides, Melakhim 10:12); but a non-Jewish litigant cannot be compelled to submit to the jurisdiction of a Jewish court, even if his non-Jewish adversary has already submitted to it (ibid.). Where non-Jews submit to the jurisdiction of a Jewish court, their causes will be determined according to their own non-Jewish law or custom, unless they expressly opt for Jewish law to be applied (Responsa attributed to Nahmanides, 225; Ritba ad *Bava Metzia* 71b).

Equal protection of the law means, first and foremost, equality in the administration of justice. The biblical injunction "injustice shalt thou judge" (Lev. 19:15) is further elaborated by the Deuteronomist as follows: "Hear the causes between your brethren, and judge righteously between every man and his brother, and the stranger that is with him. Ye shall not respect persons in judgment; but ye shall hear the small as well as the great; ye shall not be afraid of the face of man" (Deut. 1:16–17). Entering from the general into particulars, Maimonides answers the question "What is justice in the process of law?" in the following terms: "It is the equalization of both parties for all purposes: not that one should be allowed to speak as he pleases and the other be cut short; not that one be treated with courtesy and the other with irritation; and if one is dressed well and the other is dressed poorly, the welldressed is to be asked either to dress as the other or to dress the other as himself, before the case is heard; not that one should stand and the other be seated, or that one should sit above and the other sit below, but both should stand or sit next to each other" (Maimonides, *Sanhedrin* 21:1–3, restating *Sifra, Kedoshim* 4; BT *Sanhedrin* 6:2; BT *Shevu'ot* 30a). The rule of the equality of litigants was later pushed to the extreme of disallowing several plaintiffs to sue a single defendant, or one plaintiff to sue several defendants, in the same action (Mordekhai ad *Shevu'ot* 4:761).

The biblical commands not to be a respecter of persons and not to discriminate between rich and poor (above, and Deut. 16:19, Exod. 23:3) are, of course, but another aspect of the same rule of equality. But as nature has made men unequal, the doctrine of equality had to be modified to fit realities: the equality of all men before the law can only mean that, *ceteris paribus*, nobody is to be preferred and nobody is to be slighted. The necessary reservation, "all other things being equal," opens the door to legitimate inequalities, but each such departure from equality is derived from other rules of justice likewise equally valid for all. Thus we find, immediately following the rule of the equality of litigants, the exception that when there are many litigants in court waiting for their cases to be heard, priority is to be given first to orphans, second to widows (cf. Isa. 1:17), third to scholars; and as between male and female litigants, priority is given to women (Maimonides, *Sanhedrin* 21:6; Hoshen Mishpat 15:2). Later jurists held these priorities to be subject to an overriding priority of the litigant who came first and waited longest (Rashi ad *Sanhedrin* 8a; Hoshen Mishpat 15:1). In the cases of orphans and widows, the priority accorded to them stems from considerations of charity; in the case of scholars, from the public interest in minimizing the loss of time from their holy studies; and in the case of women, from the desire to spare them the embarrassment of having to wait in court (Maimonides, loc. cit.); and as to the waiting list, the priority stems, of course, from considerations of efficiency and fairness.[17]

Haim Cohn

Core Ethic 5

Truth and tolerance:
commitment to a culture of
tolerance and a life in
truthfulness.

Truthfulness

Leo Baeck

The commandment of the unconditional was created in Judaism. The good is the task to which a man is obligated by his God, who has created him and commands him. In every "Thou shalt" that is spoken to him there speak out the words "I am the Eternal One, your God." Thus the life of man has its "either–or," its absolute commandment; he is to go the way that is the way of God. The main decision, his choice, is called for; the demand "Begin, decide," runs through the Bible as through the religious writing that follows it. In this one thing in particular Judaism proves to be the un-ancient in antiquity; in this unconditional seriousness which is its characteristic, in this repudiation of all opportunism, in this rejection of all religious indifference and all moral neutrality, in this awareness that God commands, in this categorical quality expressed by the saying "with all your heart, with all your soul and with all your strength." Here is the root of the truthfulness which Judaism demands.

This unconditional, this categorical character of the commandment and the responsibility has grown out of belief in the one God. There is also a monotheism and a polytheism of morality. The one God is matched by the one commandment, the one moral: "You shall be wholly with the Eternal, your God." Just as there are no other gods alongside him, so there can be no other commandment alongside his; there cannot be a double morality, a double truth. Human beings have learned from belief in the one God what uprightness of soul is—and uprightness means totality, totality of will, feeling and thought. By it they have learned what religious truthfulness, what conviction is, religious, moral conviction and not merely intellectual—personal conviction of the truth which embraces the whole person, so that he lives in it and is ready to die for it. The unity of God calls for unconditional truthfulness, the decision between good and evil, between purity and perversity. "Teach me, Eternal One, Your way, I will walk in Your truth, let my heart be one, that I may fear Your name."

Thus truth is the task which is given to a person, the task of truthfulness. God is the God of truth, and man should be a man of truthfulness; he should go the straight way in purity of heart. Truth is a commandment, but not a gift; a moral obligation, but not an item of faith; a matter of conscience, but not an occasion for confession. In Judaism it possesses a moral sense and not the dogmatic character which is given to it elsewhere. In essence it is something that human beings practice, which they are to preserve and fulfill. Thus there stand alongside each other as the human ideal: "He walks straight and exercises right and speaks truth in his heart." Thus the prophet also praises it: "He walks in my precepts and preserves my laws, to do truth" (Ezek. 18:9). As always in Judaism, action comes first. And this also proves to be the case in the life of the soul. The just action begets the just idea, the right way leads to insight into the right, the work of truth leads to truthfulness, just as the crooked walk results in crooked thinking. Our action governs our judgment, we believe in what we do.

As in this way in the truth man is given a moral task, it is something that he is to show his fellow human being, in which he is to live with him; for all moral achievement becomes achievement in the neighbor. The very word in the Bible, the word *emet*, says this; for it denotes not only truth but also faithfulness; it becomes synonymous with righteousness and honesty. And the truth thus becomes something that is owed to the fellow human being. Just as in all action toward fellow human beings, in all *tzedakah*, in Judaism the principle is that he has a claim to it, so that we "withhold" it from him if we do not give it to him, so too it is with truth. It is therefore due to the fellow human being, to its most secret foundations, to the most hidden thoughts, and we commit theft—the Talmud ventured this word—against him if we violate the truth towards him; we "steal thoughts" if we are untruthful to him.

This strict view also comes about in Judaism from the fact that the truth is the commandment of God, God who sees the most secret things, "examines the heart and reins." The saying of the Talmud that "God desires the heart" also applies here. The Psalmist had already confessed it like this: "Behold, Thou desirest truth in the innermost parts." In the truth, the disposition is called on, it represents the purity and authenticity, the straightness and honesty of the soul. It is the unconditional accord of the word with the mind and the feelings, the truth which addresses one "in the heart."

In this way it has established itself in Judaism. Granted, deceit and deception are reported from the childhood days of Israel, of all those who delighted in childhood fantasy. For example the narratives of the human past include the story of the devious Jacob, and alongside that is what the Hellenic people sang about its Odysseus, rich in guile. But it is precisely here that the characteristic feature of the Israelite view becomes evident. For the characteristic thing about Jacob's life is not the guile which was able to deceive; this belongs in the story of his wanderings and changes. What gives him his importance in the biblical narratives is the moral struggle in which he fought with himself and conquered himself; it is the way that he found through that, so that he was no longer to be called Jacob, but Israel. The truth proves right, it is the answer.

It then found its ideal expression in the demand for martyrdom. It is not enough that all that we speak is truth; we are also to bear witness to the truth, we are to be ready to prove it by giving up our lives, by surrendering our existence, in order to assert it, to bring it about. In this way our truthfulness becomes action, our disposition the moral achievement which risks everything. Here again that categorical, unconditional element comes out, that commandment for a decision which is distinctive of Judaism. The truthfulness, the totality which human beings preserve in it is completed in martyrdom. Therefore martyrdom is the last fulfillment of the saying: love God with all your soul.[1]

Primary Sources

INTRODUCTION

Let not a man say, "I will observe the precepts of the Torah and occupy myself with its wisdom, in order that I may obtain all the blessings written in the Torah, or to attain life in the world to come; I will abstain from transgressions against which the Torah warns, so that I may be saved from the curses written in the Torah, or that I may not be cut off from life in the world to come." It is not right to serve God after this fashion for whoever does so, serves Him out of fear. This is not the standard set by the prophets and sages.... Whoever serves God out of love, occupies himself with the study of the Law and the fulfillment of commandments and walks in the paths of wisdom, impelled by no external motive whatsoever, moved neither by fear of calamity nor by the desire to obtain material benefits; such a man does what is truly right because it is truly right.... It was the standard of the patriarch Abraham whom God called His lover, because he served only out of love. It is the standard which God, through Moses, bids us achieve, as it is said, "And thou shalt love the Lord, thy God" (Deut. 6:5). When one loves God with the right love, he will straightaway observe all the commandments out of love. What is the love of God that is befitting? It is to love the Eternal with a great and exceeding love, so strong that one's soul shall be knit up with the love of God, and one should be continually enraptured by it, like a love-sick individual.... Even intenser should be the love of God in the hearts of those who love Him. And this love should continually possess them, even as He commanded us in the phrase, "with all thy heart and with all thy soul" (Deut. 6:5).... The ancient sages said; Peradventure, you will say, "I will study Torah, in order that I may become rich, that I may be called Rabbi, that I may receive a reward in the world to come." It is therefore said, "To love the Lord." Whatever you do, do it out of love only.[2]   *Moses Maimonides*

Keep far from a false charge; do not bring death on those who are innocent and in the right, for I will not acquit the wrongdoer.

Exodus 23:7

~

You shall not steal; you shall not deal deceitfully or falsely with one another.

Leviticus 19:11

~

At Gibeon the Lord appeared to Solomon in a dream by night; and God said, "Ask, what shall I grant you?" Solomon said, "You dealt most graciously with Your servant my father David, because he walked before You in faithfulness and righteousness and in integrity of heart. You have continued this great kindness to him by giving him a son to occupy his throne, as is now the case.... Grant, then, Your servant an understanding mind to judge Your people, to distinguish between good and bad; for who can judge this vast people of Yours?"

The Lord was pleased that Solomon had asked for this. And God said to him, "Because you asked for this—you did not ask for long life, you did not ask for riches, you did not ask for the life of your enemies, but you asked for discernment in dispensing justice—I now do as you have spoken. I grant you a wise and discerning mind; there has never been anyone like you before, nor will anyone like you arise again. And I also grant you what you did not ask for—both riches and glory all your life—the like of which no king has ever had. And I will further grant you long life, if you will walk in My ways and observe My laws and commandments, as did your father David."

Then Solomon awoke: it was a dream!

I Kings 3:5–6, 9–15

~

These are the things you are to do: Speak the truth to one another, render true and perfect justice in your gates. And do not contrive evil against one another, and do not love perjury, because all those are things that I hate—declares the Lord.

Zechariah 8:16–17

~

Lord, who may sojourn in Your tent, who may dwell on Your holy mountain? He who lives without blame, who does what is right, and in his heart acknowledges the truth.

Psalm 15:1–2

~

Ride on in the cause of truth and meekness and right.

Psalm 45:5

~

Six things the Lord hates; seven are an abomination to Him:
A haughty bearing, a lying tongue, hands that shed innocent blood, a mind that hatches evil plots, feet quick to run to evil, a false witness testifying lies, and one who incites brothers to quarrel.

Proverbs 6:16–19

~

Know, therefore, my children, that two spirits wait upon man— the spirit of truth and the spirit of deceit. And in the midst is the spirit of understanding of the mind, to which it belongeth to turn whithersoever it will. And the works of truth and the works of deceit are written upon the hearts of men, and each one of them the Lord knoweth.

And there is no time at which the works of men can be hid; for on the heart itself have they been written down before the Lord. And the spirit of truth testifieth all things, and accuseth all; and the sinner is burnt up by his own heart, and cannot raise his face to the judge.   *Testaments of the Twelve Patriarchs 4:20*

⌒

Speak truth each one with his neighbor. So shall ye not fall into wrath and confusion; but ye shall be in peace, having the God of peace, so shall no war prevail over you.

Testaments of the Twelve Patriarchs 7:5

⌒

But truth abideth, and is strong for ever; she liveth and conquereth for evermore. With her there is no accepting of persons or rewards; but she doeth the things that are just, *and refraineth* from all unrighteous and wicked things; and all men do well like of her works.   *1 Esdras 4:38–39*

⌒

How did they admonish the witnesses in capital cases? They brought them in and admonished them, [saying,] "Perchance ye will say what is but supposition or hearsay or at secondhand, or [ye may say in yourselves], We heard it from a man that was trustworthy. Or perchance ye do not know that we shall prove you by examination and inquiry? Know ye, moreover, that capital cases are not as non-capital cases: in non-capital cases a man may pay money and so make atonement, but in capital cases the witness is answerable for the blood of him [that is wrongfully condemned] and the blood of his posterity [that should have been born to him] to the end of the world. For so have we found it with Cain that slew his brother, for it is written, *"The bloods of thy brother cry."* It says not "The blood of thy brother," but *The bloods of thy brother*— his blood and the blood of his posterity.

And if perchance ye would say, Why should we be at these pains?—was it not once written, *He being a witness, whether he hath seen or known, [if he do not utter it, then shall he bear his iniquity]*?[4]

Mishnah Sanhedrin 4:5

⌒

Rabban Simeon b. Gamaliel says, "On three things the world stands: On justice, truth, and peace" (*M. Avot* 1:18). And the three of them are really one thing. If justice is carried out, truth is realized. [If truth is realized], peace is made.[5]

Jerusalem Talmud, Taanit 4:2

Raba said, When man is led in for judgment he is asked, Did you deal faithfully [i.e., with integrity], did you fix times for learning, did you engage in procreation, did you hope for salvation, did you engage in the dialectics of wisdom, did you understand one thing from another?   *Babylonian Talmud, Shabbat 31a*

Three the Holy One, blessed be He, hates: he who speaks one thing with his mouth and another thing in his heart; and he who possesses evidence concerning his neighbor and does not testify for him; and he who sees something indecent in his neighbor and testifies against him alone. As it once happened that Tobias sinned and Zigud alone came and testified against him before R. Papa, [whereupon] he had Zigud punished. "Tobias sinned and Zigud is punished!" exclaimed he, "Even so," said he to him, "for it is written, *one witness shall not rise up against a man*, whereas you have testified against him alone: you merely bring him into ill repute."

Babylonian Talmud, Pesachim 113b

Our Rabbis taught: *And thou shalt take no gift*; there was no need to speak of [the prohibition of] a gift of money, but [this was meant:] Even a bribe of words is also forbidden, for Scripture does not write, *And thou shalt take no gain*. What is to be understood by "a bribe of words"?—As the bribe offered to Samuel. He was once crossing [a river] on a board when a man came up and offered him his hand. "What," [Samuel] asked him, "is your business here?"—"I have a lawsuit," the other replied. "I," came the reply, "am disqualified from acting for you in the suit."

Babylonian Talmud, Kethubot 105b

∽

Behold, how vicious is slander! It is more vicious than murder, unchastity, and idolatry put together. In Scripture, each of these three transgressions is termed "great," but slander is spoken of in the plural as "great things." Thus, Cain said of murder, "My punishment is more great than I can bear" (Gen. 4:13); Joseph exclaimed of unchastity, "How then can I do this great wickedness?" (Gen. 39:9); Moses said of idolatry, "Oh, this people have sinned a great sin" (Exod. 32:31). But of slander it is written, "The Lord shall cut off all flattering lips, the tongue that speaketh great things" (Ps. 12:4), to tell you that slander is more vicious than the other three transgressions.[6]   *Aggadic tradition*

∽

But I praise those who love and acknowledge the truth, for the acknowledgment of the truth is dearer to God than sacrifice, while impertinently to insist on the lie and to deny truth is a criminal offence. I call people who do this "deceitful criminals" (Ezek. 13:11) and someone once said: "The truth that troubles me is dearer to me than the lie which benefits me."[7]   *Salomo ben Mose*

∽

It is forbidden to accustom oneself to smooth speech and flatteries. One must not say one thing and mean another. Inward and outward self should correspond; only what we have in mind, should we utter with the mouth. We must deceive no one, not even an idolater.... A person should always cherish truthful speech, an upright spirit and a pure heart free from all frowardness and perversity.[8]   *Moses Maimonides*

∽

I have discovered no better trait than silence.

What a wise observation! For inevitably, the more words one utters, the more one sins against some human being. And the fewer the words, the less the chances for sin.

Of course, there are various categories of speech. Some speech is purely damaging and devoid of any utility; some is partly damaging and partly careful; some is totally innocuous; some is totally useful.

I prefer to divide human speech into five categories.

The first category consists of sacred speech which God commands us. By this I mean the study of Bible, prayer, and any other verbal activities favored by Scripture.

The second is speech forbidden to us by the Bible such as false witness, lies, gossip, curses, obscenities, and slander. Slander is particularly evil: it destroys the slanderer, the listener, and the victim alike.

The third type is common speech which is neither useful nor sinful. By this I mean the normal, daily, and idle talk common to most humans. Pious people try to diminish such idle chatter.

The fourth is most desirable. It includes speech designed to exalt intellectual faculties and ethical qualities while denigrating intellectual and ethical defects. Through the techniques of stories and poems, such speech attempts to develop ethical behavior in people. It warns the listener to shun character defects; it praises virtuous people and lauds their ways so as to stir the listener to emulate their example.

The fifth category of speech is practical talk—speech connected with a person's business activities, food, drink, clothing, and other daily necessities. Such speech is morally neutral; it is neither virtuous nor evil. Nevertheless, it is best to keep such talk at a minimum. The ethical man abstains totally from prohibited or sinful talk, and he speaks but little of mundane matters. On the other hand, he speaks of divine and intellectual matters all the days of his life.

But two warnings are in order.

First, a man's deeds should harmonize with his words. Let him practice what he preaches.

Second, let a man say little and do much. Better to be a person of action rather than words.[9]

Moses Maimonides

꩜

A person is forbidden to testify in a matter of which he has no personal knowledge, even if his knowledge is based on what a reliable person had told him. If the litigant says to him: "Come to court and just stand by the one witness that I have in order to make the debtor believe that I have two witnesses and consequently he will admit his obligation to me," he must not hearken to him, as it is written (Exod. 23:7): "Keep thee far from a false matter."[10]

Kitzur Shulchan Arukh 181:12

꩜

Do not taunt your neighbor. This means that you must neither do nor say to him that which might shame him, though there be no one else present.... To insult one's neighbor in the presence of others is an even graver sin.... Concerning the giving of misleading advice, we learn in the *Sifra* that in the commandment, "Thou shalt not put a stumbling block before the blind," the term "blind" refers to one who is in the dark concerning any matter.... If your neighbor seeks advice, do not give such advice as may him harm. Say not, "Sell your field," if your object is to get possession of the field. You may think, "I have given him good advice." Yet in your heart you know whether you are sincere, as it is said (Lev. 19:14), "Thou shalt fear thy God" (*Sifra* to Lev. 19:14).[11]

Moses Hayyim Luzzatto

꩜

Our Sages long ago stated the general rule that "everyone is guilty of a modicum of the sin of slander" (B. B. 165a). What constitutes a modicum of slander? When, for instance, we say of someone,

"He is a man whose hearth fires are always burning" ('Arak. 15b),
or when we enumerate a man's virtues in the presence of his enemies ('Arak. 16a). Such remarks, however unimportant and far
removed from slander they may seem, actually partake of its character. Know for a rule that the *Yezer* is resourceful. So that, to
make any remark which is apt to cause injury or disgrace to one's
neighbor, whether in his presence or in his absence, is to commit
slander, a sin which is hateful and abominable to the Lord.
"Whoever makes a habit of speaking slander," say our Sages, "acts
as though he denied the existence of God" ('Arak. 15b). And in
Scripture we read, "Whoso slandereth his neighbor in secret, him
will I destroy" (Ps. 101:5).[12]

Moses Hayyim Luzzatto

Someone who pretends that his neighbor's work is his own is like
one who commits adultery.[13]

Nachman of Breslov

Thus truthfulness in itself is justice's highest demand, and lies are
in themselves a crime, which destroy others as well as yourself.
But for the whole of life's purity, the consequences of the habit of
lying are as horrible as are blissful the consequences of truthfulness.... In accordance with the commandment "Keep thee far
from a false matter," our wise men warn us expressly against supporting another person's lie even if only by remaining silent oneself or by the mere fact of one's presence; by standing silently by
while another gives expression to a falsehood; by lying, even if it
is intended to support a truth, etc.[14]

Samson Raphael Hirsch

The cohesion of religion and rational knowledge is the secure
ground for the virtue of truthfulness in all human concerns,

particularly in all questions of science and in all problems of inquiry. Truthfulness presupposes a foundation of truth upon which it rests. For the systematic connection of all the questions of knowledge, God is the principle of truth. For the particular kinds of knowledge this root of truth has as its offshoots the particular principles of method. Thus, for ethics the general principle of the moral law becomes this offshoot of the truth. Without this principle, ethics deteriorates to skepticism and sophistry, which abolish the objective foundation of truthfulness. For politics as well as for private life, morality then becomes an illusion or a matter of expediency. The condition of the truth, which ethics claims on the basis of its method, saves for it the privilege of truthfulness. If in religion God is elevated to the absolute foundation of truth, then accordingly its fundamental meaning for the security of human truthfulness is also increased....

The duty of truthfulness is enjoined in the Pentateuch by the prohibition of lying. Moreover, the lie is also called falsehood and fraud. "Keep thee far from a false word" (Exod. 23:7). This sentence is preceded by the prohibition of refusing assistance to the enemy when his ass succumbs under his burden and, further, the prohibition of favoring a poor man in his cause. The prohibition of lying is followed by other prescriptions concerning the administration of justice, and in this negative form the prohibition is also connected with the other word for lying (Lev. 19:11). However, it is also said positively: "Speak the truth one to another" (Zech. 7:9). The psalms are more than full of aversion to lying: "let the lying lips be dumb" (Ps. 31:19). "Deliver my soul from lying lips" (Ps. 120:2). "Every false way I hate" (Ps. 119:128). "He that speaketh falsehood shall not be established before Mine eyes" (Ps. 101:7). Finally the wonderful word to the hero: "Ride on, in behalf of truth" (Ps. 45:5). Proverbs also enjoin truthfulness: "The lip of truth shall be established forever" (Prov. 12:19). "Buy the truth and sell it not" (Prov. 23:23). "Lying lips are an abomination to the Eternal" (Prov. 12:22). The following are also wonderful: "Truth springeth out of the earth" (Ps. 85:12); and "Thou desireth truth in the inward" (Ps. 51:8). The prophets lament injustice in the land in their lamentation about falsehood and deceit. Truth is thereby connected with justice, and negatively, also with love. "No truth and no justice" (Hos. 4:1). Everywhere in the Scripture truthfulness is considered the foundation of piety.

The regard for law, which requires the testimony of a witness and an oath, was connected with religious awe for God. The oath was administered with the invocation of his name, in order to strengthen the duty of truthfulness through this judicial form of declaration. "Ye shall not swear by My name falsely" (Lev. 19:12). According to the rabbinic understanding, this prohibition is made by the third of the Ten Commandments....

However, truthfulness is also based on the personality of man himself, which is represented by the soul, which in turn is represented by honor. Honor itself, however, is only the expression of the worth, the dignity of man. The lie falsifies the honor of the speaker, of the man who in his speech testifies to his soul.[15]

Hermann Cohen

The origin of all conflict between me and my fellow men is that I do not say what I mean, and that I do not do what I say.[16]

Martin Buber

Core Ethic 6

Equal rights: commitment
to a culture of equal
rights and a partnership
between men and women.

Standing Again at Sinai

Judith Plaskow

At the same time, however, that the suppression of women is a real and significant aspect of Jewish life, it is just one side of Jewish women's situation. It is also the case that control of women's agency and spirituality never has been wholly effective. Though women's roles have been restricted and rendered invisible, women have in fact functioned as actors and have found outlets for their spirituality in licit and illicit places. The identification of normative Jewishness with maleness has had a profound effect on women. Yet it cannot alter the fact that Jews are men and women, and we can know Israel and its history only by looking at the experience of both.

To redefine Israel from a feminist perspective, we must incorporate the reality of women's presence into the understanding and practice of the Jewish people so that women's contributions to Jewish community are not driven underground, thwarted, or distorted, and men's are not given more weight and status than they ought to enjoy. Until that happens, both our concept of Israel and the dynamics of Jewish life will remain thoroughly misshapen by sexism. The contributions of women to Judaism will continue to be passed over in silence. Women's roles in the community will be limited, our spirituality constricted, our activity forced to find its way around blockages or to define itself over against traditional restrictions. Male activity and spirituality will continue to enjoy a false universality and normativeness that distort our understanding of Jewishness and further disguise and limit women's participation. And the Jewish community as a whole will remain deprived of its full history, and of the energy, interplay, and creative differences of its members.

These dynamics are entrenched and complexly interwoven. Yet, on the theoretical level at least, it appears fairly easy to imagine a way around them. Ostensibly, the goal of Jewish feminism is precisely the equality between men and women that would throw off the limitations placed on women and allow us to take our place beside men as full participants in Jewish life. The subordination of women is the center of the feminist critique of Judaism, and access for women to Jewish institutions and ceremonies is the basic feminist demand. There may be numerous practical impediments to achieving this end, but on a conceptual level, the goal seems clear. How can the equality of women now a fact in many individual Jewish communities become the norm in Jewish life? How can women in any individual congregation organize effectively to gain access to roles from which they have been excluded? Are there ways to reinterpret particular legal impediments to women's participation in and leadership of Jewish ritual? What are the best ways to encourage and facilitate halakhic change? Will the Orthodox community ever allow women a fuller role, and what steps might lead to desired reforms?

But while feminists need to address the concrete obstacles to women's involvement in Jewish life, and Israel needs to change in the world and not only on paper, restructuring the nature of Israel is conceptually less simple than the goal of equal access makes it seem. Equality cannot be the central feminist aim, for equality assumes as given the system in which women are to be equal. Women joining egalitarian minyanim often take for granted the content of weekly worship. Women fighting for equal rights in the public Jewish forum do not necessarily question the sexual division of spheres that undergirds women's marginalization. Women striving for halakhic change generally assume the legitimacy and authority of *halakhah*. Women as individual Jews seeking entry into a male-defined system do not necessarily look at the ways in which the Otherness of women as a class has shaped the development of Judaism from its origins.

If we are to take seriously, however, the importance of community in human life, we cannot repeat in relation to Judaism the liberal feminist mistake of seeing women as individuals who happen to be discriminated against in the Jewish system. If women fight for equality on liberal terms, then we will gain access to a community that structures its central ideas and institutions around male norms, without changing the character of those ideas or institutions. Women in Judaism—like women in any patriarchal culture—are rendered invisible *as a class*; we are seen as Other *as a class*; we are deprived of agency *as a class*. Until we understand and change the ways in which Judaism as a system supports the subordination of Jewish women as a subcommunity within the Jewish people, genuine equality of women and men is impossible.

The real challenge of feminism to Judaism emerges, not when women as individual Jews demand equal participation in the male tradition, but when women demand equality *as Jewish women*, as the class that has up until now been seen as Other. To phrase the feminist challenge to Judaism in an other than liberal way, we might say that the central issue in the feminist redefinition of Israel is the place of difference in community. Judaism can absorb many women rabbis, teachers, and communal leaders; it can ignore or change certain laws and make adjustments around the edges; it can live with the ensuing contradictions and tensions without fundamentally altering its self-understanding. But when women, with our own history and spirituality and attitudes and experiences, demand equality in a community that will allow itself to be changed by our differences, when we ask that our memories become part of Jewish memory and our presence change the present, then we make a demand that is radical and transforming. Then we begin the arduous experiment of trying to create a Jewish community in which difference is neither hierarchalized nor tolerated but truly honored. Then we begin to struggle for the only equality that is genuine.[1]

Primary Sources

INTRODUCTION

When a man marries a woman, whether virgin or nonvirgin, whether adult or minor, whether a daughter of Israel, a proselyte, or an emancipated bondswoman, he obligates himself to her for ten things. Of the ten, three are found in the Torah: *her food, her raiment, and her conjugal rights* (Exod. 21:10). *Her food* signifies her maintenance; *her raiment*, what the term implies; *her conjugal rights*, sexual intercourse with her, according to the way of the world.

The other seven are of Scribal origin, and all of them are conditions laid down by the court. The first of them is the statutory ketubbah; the rest are called "conditions contained in the ketubbah." They are the following: to treat her if she falls ill; to ransom her if she is captured; to bury her if she dies; to provide for her maintenance out of his estate; to let her dwell in his house after his death for the duration of her widowhood; to let her daughters sired by him receive their maintenance out of his estate after his death, until they become espoused; to let her male children sired by him inherit her ketubbah, in addition to their share with their half-brothers in his estate.[2]

Moses Maimonides

And God created man in His image, in the image of God He created him; male and female He created them.

Genesis 1:27

Hence a man leaves his father and mother and clings to his wife, so that they become one flesh.   *Genesis 2:24*

The daughters of Zelophehad, of Manassite family—son of Hepher son of Gilead son of Machir son of Manasseh son of Joseph—came forward. The names of the daughters were Mahlah, Noah, Hoglah, Milcah, and Tirzah. They stood before Moses, Eleazar the priest, the chieftains, and the whole assembly, at the entrance of the Tent of Meeting, and they said, "Our father died in the wilderness. He was not one of the faction, Korah's faction, which banded together against the Lord, but died for his own sin; and he has left no sons. Let not our father's name be lost to his clan just because he had no son! Give us a holding among our father's kinsmen!"

Moses brought their case before the Lord.

And the Lord said to Moses, "The plea of Zelophehad's daughters is just: you should give them a hereditary holding among their father's kinsmen; transfer their father's share to them.

"Further, speak to the Israelite people as follows: 'If a man dies without leaving a son, you shall transfer his property to his daughter.'"   *Numbers 27:1–8*

◦

When you take the field against your enemies, and the Lord your God delivers them into your power and you take some of them captive, and you see among the captives a beautiful woman and you desire her and would take her to wife, you shall bring her into your house, and she shall trim her hair, pare her nails, and discard her captive's garb. She shall spend a month's time in your house lamenting her father and mother; after that you may come to her and possess her, and she shall be your wife. Then, should you no longer want her, you must release her outright. You must not sell her for money: since you had your will of her, you must not enslave her.   *Deuteronomy 21:10–14*

◦

He who finds a wife has found happiness and has won the favor of the Lord.   *Proverbs 18:22*

～

What a rare find is a capable wife! Her worth is far beyond that of rubies. Her husband puts his confidence in her, and lacks no good thing. She is good to him, never bad, all the days of her life.

Proverbs 31:10–12

～

But when woman too had been made, beholding a figure like his own and a kindred form, he was gladdened by the sight, and approached and greeted her. She, seeing no living thing more like herself than he, is filled with glee and shamefastly returns his greeting. Love supervenes, brings together and fits into one the divided halves, as it were, of a single living creature, and sets up in each of them a desire for fellowship with the other with a view to the production of their like.[3]

Philo of Alexandria

～

When the daughters of Zelophehad (Num. 27:1–12) heard that the land was being divided among men to the exclusion of women, they assembled together to take counsel. They said: "The compassion of God is not as the compassion of men. The compassion of men extends to men more than to women, but not thus is the compassion of God; His compassion extends equally to men and women and to all, even as it is said, 'The Lord is good to all, and His mercies are over all his works'" (Ps. 145:9).[4]

Sifre Numeri

～

Thus said Rab in the name of R. Reuben b. Estrobile, from the Torah, from the Prophets and from the Hagiographa it may be shown that a woman is [destined to] a man by God. From the Torah: *Then Laban and Bethuel answered and said, The thing proceedeth from the Lord.* From the Prophets: *But his* [Samson's] *father and mother knew not that it was of the Lord.* And from the

Hagiographa: *House and riches are the inheritance of fathers, but a prudent wife is from the Lord.*

Babylonian Talmud, Mo'ed Katan 18b

~

Our Rabbis taught: Concerning a man who loves his wife as himself, who honors her more than himself, who guides his sons and daughters in the right path and arranges for them to be married near the period of their puberty, Scripture says, *And thou shalt know that thy tent is in peace.* *Babylonian Talmud, Yevamot 62b*

~

R. Eleazar said: Any man who has no wife is no proper man; for it is said, *Man and female created He them and called their name Adam.* *Babylonian Talmud, Yevamot 63a*

~

R. Helbo said: One must always observe the honor due to his wife, because blessings rest on a man's home only on account of his wife, for it is written, *And he treated Abram well for her sake.*

Babylonian Talmud, Bava Metzia 59a

~

"Be of the disciples of Aaron, loving peace" (*Aboth* 1:12). If a man quarrelled with his wife, and the husband turned the wife out of the house, then Aaron would go to the husband and say, "My son, why did you quarrel with your wife?" The man would say, "Because she acted shamefully towards me." Aaron would reply, "I will be your pledge that she will not do so again." Then he would go to the wife, and say to her, "My daughter, why did you quarrel with your husband?" And she would say, "Because he beat me and cursed me." Aaron would reply, "I will be your pledge that he will not beat you or curse you again." Aaron would do this day after day until the husband took her back. Then in due course the wife would have a child, and she would say, "It is only through the merit of Aaron that this son has been given to me" [and she would call the boy Aaron]. Some say that there were more than three thousand Israelites called Aaron. And so, when Aaron died, it says that all the congregation mourned for him. But when Moses died, it says that those who wept were the children of Israel, not all the children of Israel (Num. 20:29; Deut. 34:8).[5]

Avot de Rabbi Natan

~

In the past, Adam was created from the ground, and Eve from Adam; but henceforth it shall be, In our image, after our likeness (Gen. 1:26): neither man without woman nor woman without man, nor both of them without the *Shechinah*.[6]

Midrash Genesis Rabbah

~

Rabbi Aha said: If a man marries a godly wife, it is as though he had fulfilled the whole Torah from beginning to end. To him applies, "Thy wife is like a fruitful vine" (Ps. 128:3). Therefore the verses of the chapter of the virtuous wife in Proverbs (ch. 31) are arranged in complete alphabetical sequence (and no letter is missing, as in other alphabets in the Bible) from Alef to Tau. It is solely for the merit of the righteous women in each generation that each generation is redeemed, as it is said, "He remembers His lovingkindness and faithfulness by reason of the house of Israel" (Ps. 98:3). It does not say "by reason of the children of Israel", but "by reason of the house of Israel".[7]

Midrash Rut Zuta

~

A [Roman] noblewoman asked R. Yose ben Halafta, "In how many days did the Holy One create His world?" R. Yose replied, "In six days." She asked, "And what has He been doing since?" R. Yose replied, "The Holy One has been busy making matches: the daughter of So-and-so to So-and-so." The noblewoman said, "If that is all He does, I can do the same thing. How many menservants, how many maidservants do I have! In no time at all, I can match them up." R. Yose: "Matchmaking may be a trivial thing in your eyes; but for the Holy One, it is as awesome an act as splitting the Red Sea."

R. Yose ben Halafta left the noblewoman and went away. What did she do? She took a thousand menservants and a thousand maidservants, lined them up in row upon row facing one another, and said, "This man shall marry that woman, and this woman shall be married to that man," and so she matched them all up in a single night. In the morning, the ones thus matched came to the lady, one with his head bloodied, one with his eye knocked out, one with his shoulder dislocated, and another with his leg broken. She asked, "What happened to you?" One replied, "I don't want that woman," and another replied, "I don't want that man."

The noblewoman promptly sent to have R. Yose ben Halafta brought to her. She said to him, "Master, your Torah is completely right, excellent and worthy of praise. All you said is exactly so."[8]

Aggadic tradition

⁓

One time Alexander told his sages: I want to go to the province of Africa. Presently he came to Carthage, a realm inhabited only by women. He was about to make war against them. But they said to him: If you slay us, people will say that he killed women; and if we slay you, they will speak of you as the king whom women killed. So he said: Bring me bread. They brought him bread of gold and apples and pomegranates of gold placed upon a golden table. He asked them: Do people in your realm eat bread of gold? They replied: If you wanted bread, did you have no bread in your own country, that you had to bestir yourself and come here?

When he left, he wrote on the gate of the city: "I, Alexander of Macedon, was a fool until I came to Carthage and learned good counsel from women."[9]

Aggadic tradition

⌒

The sages of the school of R. Eliezer taught: In the verse "These are the ordinances which Thou shalt set before them" (Exod. 21:1), Scripture makes a woman equal to a man in regard to all the ordinances governing relations between one person and another.

The sages of the school of R. Ishmael taught: In the verse "When a man or woman commit any sin" (Num. 5:6), Scripture makes a woman equal to a man in regard to all penalties prescribed in the Torah.[10]   *Aggadic tradition*

⌒

A woman may not be betrothed except with her consent, and if one betrothes her against her will, she is not betrothed. On the other hand, if a man is coerced into betrothing a woman against his will, she is betrothed.[11]   *Moses Maimonides*

⌒

The Sages have further enacted that a wife's earnings are chargeable against her maintenance, her ransom against the usufruct of her estate, and her burial expenses against the husband's inheritance of her ketubbah.

Therefore, if the wife says, "I want neither maintenance nor work," her wish must be respected and she may not be coerced. On the other hand, if the husband says, "I will neither support you nor take any of your earnings," no attention need be paid to him, perchance her earnings will not suffice for her support. It is because of this enactment that the obligation of maintenance is regarded as one of the conditions contained in the ketubbah.[12]
                                                                    Moses Maimonides

⌒

If she says, "I have come to loathe him, and I cannot willingly submit to his intercourse," he must be compelled to divorce her immediately, for she is not like a captive woman who must submit

to a man that is hateful to her. She must, however, leave with for-
feiture of all of her ketubbah, but may take her worn-out clothes
that are still on hand, regardless of whether they are part of the
property brought by her to her husband, for which he had become
surety, or are melog property, for which he had not become surety.[13]

Moses Maimonides

A father is required to teach his daughters *mitzvot* and halachic
rules. Now you may ask, "How does this square with the statement of the rabbis, 'Whoever teaches his daughter Torah teaches
her obscenity'?" The rabbis have in mind the teaching of in-depth
Talmudic studies, the analysis of *mitzvot*, and the mystical aspects
of the Torah. These should not be taught to women. But the practical laws of *mitzvot* should be taught to women, because if a
woman does not know these, how is she to observe Shabbat or any
other *mitzvah*? In the days of King Hezekiah, both men and
women, adults and children alike were well-versed even in the
laws of *Taharot* (purity) and *Kodashim* (sacrifices).[14]

Yehudah HeChasid

We can hold firm to our dear Torah but we human beings have
been given the choice to be able to do what we want. And in the
Torah it is written about reward and punishment for good and evil
deeds: "But choose life."[15]

Glückel of Hamelin

How different [as among the Greeks] is it [the position of
women] in Judaism! At the very beginning we find the idea
expressed, "Man leaves his father and his mother, and unites himself with his wife, and they become one flesh,"—*an essential unity*.
The reverence due to parents, however deeply rooted, however
fervently nurtued and cultivated, is secondary to the ardent

attachment that should bind man and wife together. The wife shall follow her husband: "To thy husband shall be thy desire, and he shall rule over thee"; nevertheless, she shall be his equal in all respects; he unites himself to his wife, and they become *one* being.[16]

Abraham Geiger

~

The woman is highly prized in Israel, she is to be the priestess of the house. If our law does not assign to her a part in the public life of the people, it gives her a high position in the home, in the sphere of her vocation, it demands of the husband deep love, regard and respect toward her, and says: he who loves his wife like himself and honors her more than himself, only such a one fulfills his duty as a husband. The wife should be the holiest possession of the husband, he should belong only to her and to his home with every object that he acquires, with every faculty that he possesses, with every joy that comes to him, with his whole being. The husband should see in his wife the being who perfects his manhood, the great central pillar of his household, the better part of himself; he should love her as such and honor her and remain true to her, as the creator of her life's joys, as her masculine support in life's journey, her shield, protection and strength.[17]

Samson Raphael Hirsch

~

There is no distinct word for friendship in classical Hebrew. Friendship is, rather, the original form of love. Therefore it is also possible to say that there is no distinct word for love. Love is, rather, love of one's fellowman, which can be only friendship. To this are added now man's love for God and even God's love for men. This reciprocal relation, too, is based on friendship, on the brotherhood of the covenant. In the last analysis everything is nothing other than faithfulness, which now becomes friendship, now love in its different forms, but never becomes any other thing; rather, it remains faithfulness.

Love, in the special form of sexual love, leads to marriage, to the marriage bond. This bond is not a fetter. Therefore marriage, according to Jewish law, can be dissolved when moral requirements invalidate the assumptions of the marriage. Precisely the legal possibility of divorce shows faithfulness to be the meaning and foundation of the marriage bond.

The purpose of marriage is to establish a unity of consciousness above and beyond the changing impulse of sexual love, even on this borderline of sexual passion. Education and habituation to faithfulness is the meaning of marriage. Without this meaning, marriage would merely be an institution for child bearing, and any other purpose would be a vain illusion. For any such purpose, faithfulness is indeed a physiological hindrance since change heightens desire. If, however, for the consorts themselves marriage has its validity in their mutual spiritual well-being, then this mutual relationship is based exclusively on the ideal of faithfulness, which is the task of marriage....

Jewish marriage law has confirmed this meaning by making the consecration of the marriage an act of divine worship. Moreover, rabbinical legislation has sought to protect in various ways the honor of the wife against the legal authority of the husband, so that the monogamous character of marriage is beyond question, although, because of the original oriental conditions, a certain indulgence in this case also could not be avoided. Nonetheless, among all the historical documents of Jewish morality, the Jewish marriage is foremost in testifying that faithfulness is a characteristic trait of the Jewish mind. Here, too, the last chapter of the Proverbs, with its hymn to the courageous woman, serves as a poetic testimony to faithfulness.[18]

Hermann Cohen

When G-d told Moshe to prepare the Jews to receive the Torah, He commanded him, "This is what you shall say to the House of Yaakov and speak to the children of Israel." Our Sages explain that the

"House of Yaakov" refers to Jewish women, and "the children of Israel," to the men; i.e., G-d told Moshe to approach the women first.

This order implies a sense of priority. For Torah to be perpetuated among the Jewish people, precedence must be given to Jewish women. Giving such prominence to women may appear questionable in view of several traditional attitudes. Those attitudes, however, are narrow and restrictive when judged by the objective standard of Torah law and certainly may be considered so within the context of the application of these standards to contemporary society.

Torah law requires a woman to study all the laws and concepts necessary to observe the commandments which she is obligated to fulfill. This encompasses a vast scope of knowledge, including the laws of Shabbat, keeping kosher and Family Purity, and many other areas of Jewish law. Indeed, many men would be happy if their Torah knowledge would be as complete.

Also, among the subjects which a woman must know is *Pnimiyus HaTorah*, Torah's mystic dimension. A woman is obligated to fulfill the commandment of knowing G-d, loving Him, fearing Him, and the like. Indeed, the obligation to fulfill these commandments is constant, incumbent upon us every moment of the day. The fulfillment of these commandments is dependent on the knowledge of spiritual concepts as implied by the verse, "Know the G-d of your fathers and serve Him with a full heart." The study of the inner dimension of Torah is necessary to achieve this knowledge.

Throughout the generations, we have seen women with immense Torah knowledge. The Talmud mentions Bruriah, the daughter of Rabbi Chaninah ben Tradyon and the wife of Rabbi Meir. Throughout the Middle Ages, we find records of many women who corrected their husbands' Torah texts. In his memoirs, the Previous Rebbe describes how the Alter Rebbe's family put a special emphasis on women's Torah knowledge and the Previous Rebbe educated his own daughters in this spirit.[19]

Menachem Mendel Schneerson

~

There is a double sense in which one can say that Judaism needs to be engendered. Progressive Jews understand Judaism as an evolving system, constantly reshaped and renewed through its relations with its changing historical contexts. Consequently, they would agree that a truly progressive Judaism must be one that consciously and continuously reengenders itself. In the second sense, however, Judaism has hardly begun to be engendered.

The progressive branches of Judaism have hardly begun to reflect and to address the questions, understandings, and obligations of both Jewish women and Jewish men. They are not yet fully attentive to the impact of gender on the texts and lived experiences of the people Israel. Until progressive Judaisms engender themselves in this second sense, they cannot engender adequate Judaisms in the first sense. That attempt has already been made, and it has failed.

Riv-Ellen Prell, an anthropologist of religion, describes how classical Reformers used the universalist, Enlightenment model of their host culture to eradicate the special status assigned women in Orthodoxy. Because "all men are created equal," Reform Judaism included women by categorizing them as "honorary men." But making women honorary men made them deviant men. It required viewing their differences from men as defects in their masculinity. As Prell demonstrates, this definition of equality not only hid discrimination that blocked women's full participation: it barred women from articulating experiences and concerns that men did not share. To enforce equality, it abolished the few women's mitzvot prescribed by Orthodoxy, making women even less visible than before. The experience of classical Reform illustrates a defect that feminist legal critiques have identified in the universalist understanding of equality. An equality predicated on ignoring the differences that constitute distinctive selves both conceals and legitimates injustice. An institution or enterprise is fully inclusive only if it includes people as the kind of people they really are.

Legal and philosophical critiques, not only by feminists, but by communitarians, both progressive and conservative, civil libertarians, and poststructuralists of every sort, ask us to reevaluate the Enlightenment universalist values of equality, autonomy, rights, and justice, values in which progressive Judaisms have invested heavily. These critiques suggest that universalist values that fail to recognize crucial differences among people create inadequate understandings of what it means to be human and, consequently, make poor guides for how human beings may live in community.

When we reassess the impact of these values on modern Judaism, Skotsl's problem emerges as the prime indicator of a larger problem caused by inadequacies in the very modernity progressive Judaisms embraced so fervently. The problem of Jewish women, then, cannot be ghettoized so that women can discuss and solve "their" problem unilaterally. As a key to the problems of modem Judaisms themselves, this issue affects all of us, women and men. Engendering Judaism, like other kinds of human engendering, requires women and men to act cooperatively.

If Judaism cannot be engendered without solving the problem of women, it is equally true that it cannot be engendered without solving the problem of *halakhah*. Without a means through which the stories and the values of Judaism can be embodied in communal praxis, how are they to be sustained by experiences? Values and stories are empty and meaningless if we lack ways to act upon them. Without concrete, sensuous, substantial experiences that bind us to live out our Judaisms together, there is nothing real to engender.

The difficulty about proposing a *halakhah* to progressive Jews is their presumption that the term, its definition, and its practice belong to Orthodoxy. We urgently need to reclaim this term because it is the authentic Jewish language for articulating the system of obligations that constitute the content of the covenant.

Halakhah belongs to liberal Jews no less than to Orthodox Jews because the stories of Judaism belong to us all. A *halakhah* is a communal praxis grounded in Jewish stories.

Ethicists, theologians, and lawyers who stress the centrality of narrative would argue that all normative systems rest upon stories. Whether the story is the Exodus from Egypt or the crucifixion and resurrection of Jesus or the forging of American independence, if we claim it as our own, we commit ourselves to be the kind of people that story demands, to translate its norms and values into a living praxis.

A praxis is more than the sum of the various practices that constitute it. *A praxis is a holistic embodiment in action at a particular time of the values and commitments inherent to a particular story.* Orthodoxy cannot have a monopoly on *halakhah*, because no form of Judaism can endure without one; there would be no way to live it out.

What happened to Judaism in modernity was that its praxis became both impoverished and fragmented. Some communal practices were taken over by the secular state. Other practices were jettisoned by congregations because they appeared foreign and "Oriental." Still others were abandoned by individuals because they had come to see themselves as "private citizens" with minimal obligations to other private citizens. It became impossible to imagine a unified way to live as a human being, a citizen, and a Jew.

A contemporary Jewish praxis would reduce our sense of fragmentation. If we had a praxis rather than a grab bag of practices, we would experience making love, making kiddush, recycling paper used at our workplace, cooking a pot of soup for a person with AIDS, dancing at a wedding, and making medical treatment decisions for a dying loved one as integrated parts of the same project: the holy transformation of our everyday reality. Furthermore, we would experience ourselves less as fragmented enactors of divergent roles in disparate spheres—public/private, ritual/ethical, religious/secular, duty/pleasure—and more as coherent Jewish personalities.

We cannot simply resurrect the old premodern praxis, because it no longer fits us in the world we now inhabit. Some of its elements are fundamentally incompatible with participation in postindustrial, democratic societies. The old praxis can be preserved intact only if we schizophrenically split off our religious lives from our secular lives and live two separate existences with two different sets of values and commitments. But the obligation to be truthful and the yearning to be whole are what made us progressive Jews in the first place. To be faithful to the covenant requires that we infuse the whole of our existence with our religious commitments. How is that to be done in our specific situation?

The secular values of equal respect, inclusivity, diversity, and pluralism obligate citizens to recognize and protect one another's integrity and well-being. Jews have obvious cause to espouse these values. At the same time, classical *halakhah* is committed to the subordination and exclusion of women in communal life. The inability of classical *halakhah* to resolve this dissonance is the paradigmatic example of its inadequacy as a praxis for Jews in modernity and leads inexorably toward challenges from Skotsl's modern incarnations.[20]

Rachel Adler

Do you want to know why people say, "Skotsl is coming"? Once upon a time the women complained to one another that in the world everything goes according to the will of the men. Only they may fulfill all the commandments, only the men are called in the synagogue, everything is always for the men. And no one takes any notice of the women. Then the women decided to turn to God himself. How? One got on top of the other, up and up, right up to heaven. Skotsl, a wise woman, who was a good speaker, was right at the top. But one of the women got a speck of dust in her nose and had to sneeze. The whole living ladder began to shake and they all fell down back to earth. All except one, Skotsl. However hard they looked for her, they could not find her. And because there was now no longer anyone who could have talked with God, things remained with the women as before and the men kept the upper hand. And they thought to themselves: Surely Skotsl got to heaven and is up there, moving the saints. At any moment Skotsl could return with the good news that women and men both mean a great deal. If not today, then perhaps tomorrow. And if somewhere an unknown woman appears and people ask "Who is she?", it could be Skotsl. And they say about that, "Skotsl is coming."[21]

A Yiddish story

A VISION OF HOPE
Religious Peace
and a Global Ethic

Hans Küng

When I published my book *Global Responsibility*[1] in 1990 I could refer to hardly any documents of world organizations on a global ethic. Only three years after the appearance of the Global Ethic Project there was the proclamation of the Declaration of the Parliament of the World's Religions toward a Global Ethic (1993), which I had the honor and burden of working out.[2] Six years later, when I was able to develop what I hope was a realistic forward-looking overall view under the title *A Global Ethic for Global Politics and Global Economics*,[3] there were already further important international documents—from the UN Commission for Global Governance, the World Commission on Culture and Development, and the InterAction Council of former heads of state and government.

It is a welcome sign of the times that today a body of experienced and completely realistic statespeople, namely those gathered in the InterAction Council, expressly supports as the basis for a global ethics the two fundamental principles "Every human being should be treated humanely!" and "What you wish done to yourself, do to others!" (Golden Rule). These are norms for all spheres of life, not just for the individual, but also for families and communities, peoples, nations, and religions.

In the report to a conference of a high-ranking expert group of the InterAction Council on the topic "World Religions as a Factor in World Politics" (Tübingen, Germany, May 2007), the recommendations included the following needs:

- To further the understanding that all religions have a core of ethical norms in common
- To develop further the awareness of a "world citizenship" and common membership of the human race through a worldwide ethical standard[4]

The basic ethical demand of the 1993 Chicago Declaration is the most elementary that can be put to human beings, yet one that is not completely self-evident: humanity, in the sense of true humanity:

> Now as before, women and men are treated inhumanely all over the world. They are robbed of their opportunities and their freedom; their human rights are trampled underfoot; their dignity is disregarded. But might does not make right! In the face of all inhumanity our religious and ethical convictions demand that every human being must be treated humanely! This means that every human being without distinction of age, sex, race, skin color, physical or mental ability, language, religion, political view, or national or social origin possesses an inalienable and untouchable dignity.

This is not just an individual but at the same time a social ethic. But on the other hand the morality of institutions depends on the integrity of persons. Therefore it is also important for the institutions and systems that some irrevocable directives should again be brought to mind. Moreover the global ethic document contains four such irrevocable directives, which occur in all religious and ethical traditions of humankind:

- Commitment to a culture of nonviolence and reverence for life
- Commitment to a culture of justice and a just economic order

- Commitment to a culture of tolerance and a life in truthfulness
- Commitment to a culture of equal rights and a partnership between men and women

Certainly, these are first of all words, and it depends on human beings, and above all those in authority, how far these principles are put into practice. But more than ever I am convinced that without an ethical will, without a moral driving force, without moral energy, the problems of the twenty-first century cannot be dealt with, indeed cannot even be tackled.

Today many people are becoming aware that from their own sources the religions can overcome the traditions of intolerance, indeed must even strive for more than mere "tolerance." The religions have an immense potential for conflict that is exploited by some religious and nonreligious people. But the religions also have no less a potential for peace, which has likewise had an effect. For it was particularly men and women with religious motivations who without violence and without bloodshed devoted themselves to a change, a radical change, in their countries: in Poland, in East Germany, in South Africa, in Central and South America, in the Philippines.

From this we are to conclude that a clash of cultures and religions must be avoided. And it can be avoided if sufficient people, men and women, and above all politicians and religious leaders, support it. That is my realistic vision of hope: no survival of humankind without peace between the nations. But no peace among the nations without peace among the religions. And no peace among the religions without dialogue between the religions. In front of the UN building in New York the bronze sculpture of a hammering smith impressively symbolizes the saying of the prophet Isaiah, "Beat swords into ploughshares" (Isa. 2:4). Young men are all ready to learn that violence may not be a means of controversy.

In this new world era Judaism in particular has a tremendous religious and ethical heritage to contribute. Therefore Rabbi

Walter Homolka and I have undertaken to make this potential for a universal ethic clear from the sources of Judaism. For there is no other people who has so much that is substantial and striking to offer for a coming shared ethic of humankind as Judaism with its ethical tradition, which respects the religious traditions and convictions of others and points to a common ethical task of human beings: the healing of the world (*tikkun olam*).

DECLARATION TOWARD A GLOBAL ETHIC

Council of the Parliament of the World's Religions, Chicago, September 1993

INTRODUCTION

The world is in agony. The agony is so pervasive and urgent that we are compelled to name its manifestations so that the depth of this pain may be made clear.

Peace eludes us—the planet is being destroyed—neighbors live in fear—women and men are estranged from each other—children die!

This is abhorrent.

We condemn the abuses of Earth's ecosystems.

We condemn the poverty that stifles life's potential; the hunger that weakens the human body; the economic disparities that threaten so many families with ruin.

We condemn the social disarray of the nations; the disregard for justice which pushes citizens to the margin; the anarchy overtaking our communities; and the insane death of children from violence. In particular we condemn aggression and hatred in the name of religion.

But this agony need not be.

It need not be because the basis for an ethic already exists. This ethic offers the possibility of a better individual and global order, and leads individuals away from despair and societies away from chaos.

We are women and men who have embraced the precepts and practices of the world's religions.

We affirm that a common set of core values is found in the teachings of the religions, and that these form the basis of a global ethic.

We affirm that this truth is already known, but yet to be lived in heart and action.

We affirm that there is an irrevocable, unconditional norm for all areas of life, for families and communities, for races, nations, and religions. There already exist ancient guidelines for human behavior which are found in the teachings of the religions of the world and which are the condition for a sustainable world order.

We declare:

We are interdependent. Each of us depends on the well-being of the whole, and so we have respect for the community of living beings, for people, animals, and plants, and for the preservation of Earth, the air, water and soil.

We take individual responsibility for all we do. All our decisions, actions, and failures to act have consequences.

We must treat others as we wish others to treat us. We make a commitment to respect life and dignity, individuality and diversity, so that every person is treated humanely, without exception. We must have patience and acceptance. We must be able to forgive, learning from the past but never allowing ourselves to be enslaved by memories of hate. Opening our hearts to one another, we must sink our narrow differences for the cause of the world community, practicing a culture of solidarity and relatedness.

We consider humankind our family. We must strive to be kind and generous. We must not live for ourselves alone, but should also serve others, never forgetting the children, the aged, the poor, the suffering, the disabled, the refugees, and the lonely. No person should ever be considered or treated as a second-class citizen, or be exploited in any way whatsoever. There should be equal partnership between men and women. We must not commit any kind of sexual immorality. We must put behind us all forms of domination or abuse.

We commit ourselves to a culture of nonviolence, respect, justice, and peace.

We shall not oppress, injure, torture, or kill other human beings, forsaking violence as a means of settling differences.

We must strive for a just social and economic order, in which everyone has an equal chance to reach full potential as a human being. We must speak and act truthfully and with compassion, dealing fairly with all, and avoiding prejudice and hatred. We must not steal. We must move beyond the dominance of greed for power, prestige, money, and consumption to make a just and peaceful world.

Earth cannot be changed for the better unless the consciousness of individuals is changed first. We pledge to increase our awareness by disciplining our minds, by meditation, by prayer, or by positive thinking. Without risk and a readiness to sacrifice there can be no fundamental change in our situation. Therefore we commit ourselves to this global ethic, to understanding one another, and to socially beneficial, peace-fostering, and nature-friendly ways of life.

We invite all people, whether religious or not, to do the same.

THE PRINCIPLES OF A GLOBAL ETHIC

Our world is experiencing a fundamental crisis: a crisis in global economy, global ecology, and global politics. The lack of a grand vision, the tangle of unresolved problems, political paralysis, mediocre political leadership with little insight or foresight, and in general too little sense for the commonweal are seen everywhere: too many old answers to new challenges.

Hundreds of millions of human beings on our planet increasingly suffer from unemployment, poverty, hunger, and the destruction of their families. Hope for a lasting peace among nations slips away from us. There are tensions between the sexes and generations. Children die, kill, and are killed. More and more countries are shaken by corruption in politics and business. It is increasingly difficult to live together peacefully in our cities because of social, racial, and ethnic conflicts, the abuse of drugs, organized crime, and even anarchy. Even neighbors often live in fear of one another. Our planet continues to be ruthlessly plundered. A collapse of the ecosystem threatens us.

Time and again we see leaders and members of religions incite aggression, fanaticism, hate, and xenophobia—even inspire and legitimize violent and bloody conflicts. Religion often is misused for purely power-political goals, including war. We are filled with disgust.

We condemn these blights and declare that they need not be. An ethic already exists within the religious teachings of the world which can counter the global distress. Of course this ethic provides no direct solution for all the immense problems of the world, but it does supply the moral foundation for a better individual and global order: a vision which can lead women and men away from despair, and society away from chaos.

We are persons who have committed ourselves to the precepts and practices of the world's religions. We confirm that there is already a consensus among the religions which can be the basis for a global ethic—a minimal fundamental consensus concerning binding values, irrevocable standards, and fundamental moral attitudes.

I. No New Global Order without a New Global Ethic!

We women and men of various religions and regions of Earth therefore address all people, religious and nonreligious. We wish to express the following convictions which we hold in common:

- We all have a responsibility for a better global order.
- Our involvement for the sake of human rights, freedom, justice, peace, and the preservation of Earth is absolutely necessary.

- Our different religious and cultural traditions must not prevent our common involvement in opposing all forms of inhumanity and working for greater humaneness.
- The principles expressed in this Global Ethic can be affirmed by all persons with ethical convictions, whether religiously grounded or not.
- As religious and spiritual persons we base our lives on an Ultimate Reality, and draw spiritual power and hope therefrom, in trust, in prayer or meditation, in word or silence. We have a special responsibility for the welfare of all humanity and care for the planet Earth. We do not consider ourselves better than other women and men, but we trust that the ancient wisdom of our religions can point the way for the future.

After two world wars and the end of the Cold War, the collapse of Fascism and Nazism, the shaking to the foundations of Communism and colonialism, humanity has entered a new phase of its history. Today we possess sufficient economic, cultural, and spiritual resources to introduce a better global order. But old and new ethnic, national, social, economic, and religious tensions threaten the peaceful building of a better world. We have experienced greater technological progress than ever before, yet we see that worldwide poverty, hunger, death of children, unemployment, misery, and the destruction of nature have not diminished but rather have increased. Many peoples are threatened with economic ruin, social disarray, political marginalization, ecological catastrophe, and national collapse.

In such a dramatic global situation humanity needs a vision of peoples living peacefully together, of ethnic and ethical groupings and of religions sharing responsibility for the care of Earth. A vision rests on hopes, goals, ideals, standards. But all over the world these have slipped from our hands. Yet we are convinced that, despite their frequent abuses and failures, it is the communities of faith who bear a responsibility to demonstrate that such hopes, ideals, and standards can be guarded, grounded, and lived. This is especially true in the modern state. Guarantees of freedom of conscience and religion are necessary, but they do not substitute for binding values, convictions, and norms, which are valid for all humans regardless of their social origin, sex, skin color, language, or religion.

We are convinced of the fundamental unity of the human family on Earth. We recall the 1948 Universal Declaration of Human Rights of the United Nations. What it formally proclaimed on the level of rights we wish to confirm and deepen here from the perspective of an ethic: the full realization of the intrinsic dignity of the human person, the inalienable freedom and equality in principle of all humans, and the necessary solidarity and interdependence of all humans with each other.

On the basis of personal experiences and the burdensome history of our planet we have learned:

- That a better global order cannot be created or enforced by laws, prescriptions, and conventions alone;
- That the realization of peace, justice, and the protection of Earth depends on the insight and readiness of men and women to act justly;
- That action in favor of rights and freedoms presumes a consciousness of responsibility and duty, and that therefore both the minds and hearts of women and men must be addressed;
- That rights without morality cannot long endure, and that there will be no better global order without a global ethic.

By a global ethic we do not mean a global ideology or a single unified religion beyond all existing religions, and certainly not the domination of one religion over all others. By a global ethic we mean a fundamental consensus on binding values, irrevocable standards, and personal attitudes. Without such a fundamental consensus on an ethic, sooner or later every community will be threatened by chaos or dictatorship, and individuals will despair.

II. A Fundamental Demand: Every Human Being Must Be Treated Humanely

We are all fallible, imperfect men and women with limitations and defects. We know the reality of evil. Precisely because of this, we feel compelled for the sake of global welfare to express what the fundamental elements of a global ethic should be—for individuals as well as for communities and organizations, for states as well as for the religions themselves. We trust that our often millennia-old religious and ethical traditions provide an ethic which is convincing and practicable for all women and men of goodwill, religious and nonreligious.

At the same time we know that our various religious and ethical traditions often offer very different bases for what is helpful and what is unhelpful for men and women, what is right and what is wrong, what is good and what is evil. We do not wish to gloss over or ignore the serious differences among the individual religions. However, they should not hinder us from proclaiming publicly those things which we already hold in common and which we jointly affirm, each on the basis of our own religious or ethical grounds.

We know that religions cannot solve the environmental, economic, political, and social problems of Earth. However they can provide what obviously cannot be attained by economic plans, political programs, or legal regulations alone: a change in the inner orientation, the whole mentality, the "hearts" of people, and a conversion from a false path to a new orientation for life. Humankind urgently needs social and ecological reforms, but it needs spiritual renewal just as urgently. As religious or spiritual persons we commit ourselves to this task. The spiritual powers of the religions can offer a fundamental sense of trust, a ground of meaning, ultimate standards, and a spiritual home. Of course religions are credible only when they eliminate those conflicts which spring from the religions themselves, dismantling mutual arrogance, mistrust, prejudice, and even hostile images, and thus demonstrate respect for the traditions, holy places, feasts, and rituals of people who believe differently.

Now as before, women and men are treated inhumanely all over the world. They are robbed of their opportunities and their freedom; their human rights are trampled underfoot; their dignity is disregarded. But might does not make right! In the face of all inhumanity our religious and ethical convictions demand that every human being must be treated humanely! This means that every human being without distinction of age, sex, race, skin color, physical or mental ability, language, religion, political view, or national or social origin possesses an inalienable and untouchable dignity, and everyone, the individual as well as the state, is therefore obliged to honor this dignity and protect it. Humans must always be the subjects of rights, must be ends, never mere means, never objects of commercialization and industrialization in economics, politics and media, in research institutes, and industrial corporations. No one stands "above good and evil"—no human being, no social class, no influential interest group, no cartel, no police apparatus, no army, and no state. On the contrary: Possessed of reason and conscience, every human is obliged to behave in a genuinely human fashion, to do good and avoid evil!

It is the intention of this Global Ethic to clarify what this means. In it we wish to recall irrevocable, unconditional ethical norms. These should not be bonds and chains, but helps and supports for people to find and realize once again their lives' direction, values, orientations, and meaning.

There is a principle which is found and has persisted in many religious and ethical traditions of humankind for thousands of years: What you do not wish done to yourself, do not do to others. Or in positive terms: What you wish done to yourself, do to others! This should be the irrevocable, unconditional norm for all areas of life, for families and communities, for races, nations, and religions.

Every form of egoism should be rejected: all selfishness, whether individual or collective, whether in the form of class thinking, racism, nationalism, or sexism. We condemn these because they prevent humans from being authentically human. Self-determination and self-realization are thoroughly legitimate so long as they are not separated from human self-responsibility and global responsibility, that is, from responsibility for fellow humans and for the planet Earth.

This principle implies very concrete standards to which we humans should hold firm. From it arise four broad, ancient guidelines for human behavior which are found in most of the religions of the world.

III. Irrevocable Directives

1. Commitment to a Culture of Nonviolence and Respect for Life
Numberless women and men of all regions and religions strive to lead lives not determined by egoism but by commitment to their fellow humans and to the world around them. Nevertheless, all over the world we find endless hatred, envy, jealousy, and violence, not only between individuals but also between social and ethnic groups, between classes, races, nations, and religions. The use of violence, drug trafficking and organized crime, often equipped with new technical possibilities, has reached global proportions. Many places still are ruled by terror "from above"; dictators oppress their own people, and institutional violence is widespread. Even in some countries where laws exist to protect individual freedoms, prisoners are tortured, men and women are mutilated, hostages are killed.

A. In the great ancient religious and ethical traditions of humankind we find the directive: You shall not kill! Or in positive terms: Have respect for life! Let us reflect anew on the consequences of this ancient directive: All people have a right to life, safety, and the free development of personality insofar as they do not injure the rights of others. No one has the right physically or psychically to torture, injure, much less kill, any other human being. And no people, no state, no race, no religion has the right to hate, to discriminate against, to "cleanse", to exile, much less to liquidate a "foreign" minority which is different in behavior or holds different beliefs.

B. Of course, wherever there are humans there will be conflicts. Such conflicts, however, should be resolved without violence within a framework of justice. This is true for states as well as for individuals. Persons who hold political power must work within the framework of a just order and commit themselves to the most nonviolent, peaceful solutions possible. And they should work for this within an international order of peace which itself has need of protection and defense against perpetrators of violence. Armament is a mistaken path; disarmament is the commandment of the times. Let no one be deceived: There is no survival for humanity without global peace!

C. Young people must learn at home and in school that violence may not be a means of settling differences with others. Only thus can a culture of nonviolence be created.

D. A human person is infinitely precious and must be unconditionally protected. But likewise the lives of animals and plants which inhabit this planet with us deserve protection, preservation, and care. Limitless exploitation of the natural foundations of life, ruthless destruction of the biosphere, and militarization of the cosmos are all outrages. As human beings we have a special responsibility—especially with a view to future generations—for Earth and the cosmos, for the air, water, and soil. We are all intertwined together in this cosmos and we are all dependent on each other. Each one of us depends on the welfare of all. Therefore the dominance of humanity over nature and the cosmos must not be encouraged. Instead we must cultivate living in harmony with nature and the cosmos.

E. To be authentically human in the spirit of our great religious and ethical traditions means that in public as well as in private life we must be concerned for others and ready to help. We must never be ruthless and brutal. Every people, every race, every religion must show tolerance and respect—indeed high appreciation—for every other. Minorities need protection and support, whether they be racial, ethnic, or religious.

2. Commitment to a Culture of Solidarity and a Just Economic Order: Numberless men and women of all regions and religions strive to live their lives in solidarity with one another and to work for authentic fulfillment of their vocations. Nevertheless, all over the world we find endless hunger, deficiency, and need. Not only individuals, but especially unjust institutions and structures are responsible for these tragedies. Millions of people are without work; millions are exploited by poor wages, forced to the edges of society, with their possibilities for the future destroyed. In many lands the gap between the poor and the rich, between the powerful and the powerless is immense. We live in a world in which totalitarian state socialism as well as unbridled capitalism have hollowed out and destroyed many ethical and spiritual values. A materialistic mentality breeds greed for unlimited profit and a grasping for endless plunder. These demands claim more and more of the community's resources without obliging the individual to contribute more. The cancerous social evil of corruption thrives in the developing countries and in the developed countries alike.

A. In the great ancient religious and ethical traditions of humankind we find the directive: You shall not steal! Or in positive terms: Deal honestly and fairly! Let us reflect anew on the consequences of this ancient directive: No one has the right to rob or dispossess in any way whatsoever any other person or the commonweal. Further, no one has the right to use her or his possessions without concern for the needs of society and Earth.

B. Where extreme poverty reigns, helplessness and despair spread, and theft occurs again and again for the sake of survival. Where power and wealth are accumulated ruthlessly, feelings of envy, resentment, and deadly hatred and rebellion inevitably well up in the disadvantaged and marginalized. This leads to a vicious circle of violence and counterviolence. Let no one be deceived: There is no global peace without global justice!

C. Young people must learn at home and in school that property, limited though it may be, carries with it an obligation, and that its uses should at the same time serve the common good. Only thus can a just economic order be built up.

D. If the plight of the poorest billions of humans on this planet, particularly women and children, is to be improved, the world economy must be structured more justly. Individual good deeds, and assistance projects, indispensable though they be, are insufficient. The participation of all states and the authority of international organizations are needed to build just economic institutions. A solution which can be supported by all sides must be sought for the debt crisis and the poverty of the dissolving second world, and even more the third world. Of course conflicts of interest are unavoidable. In the developed countries, a distinction must be made between necessary and limitless consumption, between socially beneficial and nonbeneficial uses of property, between justified and unjustified uses of natural resources, and between a profit-only and a socially beneficial and ecologically oriented market economy. Even the developing nations must search their national consciences.

   Wherever those ruling threaten to repress those ruled, wherever institutions threaten persons, and wherever might oppresses right, we are obligated to resist—whenever possible nonviolently.

E. To be authentically human in the spirit of our great religious and ethical traditions means the following:

- We must utilize economic and political power for service to humanity instead of misusing it in ruthless battles for domination.
- We must develop a spirit of compassion with those who suffer, with special care for the children, the aged, the poor, the disabled, the refugees, and the lonely.
- We must cultivate mutual respect and consideration, so as to reach a reasonable balance of interests, instead of thinking only of unlimited power and unavoidable competitive struggles.
- We must value a sense of moderation and modesty instead of an unquenchable greed for money, prestige, and consumption. In greed humans lose their "souls", their freedom, their composure, their inner peace, and thus that which makes them human.

3. Commitment to a Culture of Tolerance and a Life in Truthfulness
Numberless women and men of all regions and religions strive to lead lives of honesty and truthfulness. Nevertheless, all over the world we find endless lies, and deceit, swindling and hypocrisy, ideology and demagoguery:

- Politicians and business people who use lies as a means to success
- Mass media which spread ideological propaganda instead of accurate reporting, misinformation instead of information, cynical commercial interest instead of loyalty to the truth
- Scientists and researchers who give themselves over to morally questionable ideological or political programs or to economic interest groups, or who justify research which violates fundamental ethical values
- Representatives of religions who dismiss other religions as of little value and who preach fanaticism and intolerance instead of respect and understanding

A. In the great ancient religious and ethical traditions of humankind we find the directive: You shall not lie! Or in positive terms: Speak and act truthfully! Let us reflect anew on the consequences of this ancient directive: No woman or man, no institution, no state or church or religious community has the right to speak lies to other humans.

B. This is especially true:

- For those who work in the mass media, to whom we entrust the freedom to report for the sake of truth and to whom we thus grant the office of guardian. They do not stand above morality but have the obligation to respect human dignity, human rights, and fundamental values. They are duty-bound to objectivity, fairness, and the preservation of human dignity. They have no right to intrude into individuals' private spheres, to manipulate public opinion, or to distort reality;

- For artists, writers, and scientists, to whom we entrust artistic and academic freedom. They are not exempt from general ethical standards and must serve the truth;

- For the leaders of countries, politicians, and political parties, to whom we entrust our own freedoms. When they lie in the faces of their people, when they manipulate the truth, or when they are guilty of venality or ruthlessness in domestic or foreign affairs, they forsake their credibility and deserve to lose their offices and their voters. Conversely, public opinion should support those politicians who dare to speak the truth to the people at all times;

- Finally, for representatives of religion. When they stir up prejudice, hatred, and enmity toward those of different belief, or even incite or legitimize religious wars, they deserve the condemnation of humankind and the loss of their adherents. Let no one be deceived: There is no global justice without truthfulness and humaneness!

C. Young people must learn at home and in school to think, speak, and act truthfully. They have a right to information and education to be able to make the decisions that will form their lives. Without an ethical formation they will hardly be able to distinguish the important from the unimportant. In the daily flood of information, ethical standards will help them discern when opinions are portrayed as facts, interests veiled, tendencies exaggerated, and facts twisted.

D. To be authentically human in the spirit of our great religious and ethical traditions means the following:

- We must not confuse freedom with arbitrariness or pluralism with indifference to truth.
- We must cultivate truthfulness in all our relationships instead of dishonesty, dissembling, and opportunism.
- We must constantly seek truth and incorruptible sincerity instead of spreading ideological or partisan half-truths.
- We must courageously serve the truth and we must remain constant and trustworthy, instead of yielding to opportunistic accommodation to life.

4. Commitment to a Culture of Equal Rights and a Partnership between Men and Women: Numberless men and women of all regions and religions strive to live their lives in a spirit of partnership and responsible action in the areas of love, sexuality, and family. Nevertheless, all over the world there are condemnable forms of patriarchy, domination of one sex over the other, exploitation of women, sexual misuse of children, and forced prostitution. Too frequently, social inequities force women and even children into prostitution as a means of survival—particularly in less developed countries.

A. In the great ancient religious and ethical traditions of humankind we find the directive: You shall not commit sexual immorality! Or in positive terms: Respect and love one another! Let us reflect anew on the consequences of this ancient directive: No one has the right to degrade others to mere sex objects, to lead them into or hold them in sexual dependency.

B. We condemn sexual exploitation and sexual discrimination as one of the worst forms of human degradation. We have the duty to resist wherever the domination of one sex over the other is preached—even in the name of religious conviction; wherever sexual exploitation is tolerated, wherever prostitution is fostered or children are misused. Let no one be deceived: There is no authentic humaneness without a living together in partnership!

C. Young people must learn at home and in school that sexuality is not a negative, destructive, or exploitative force, but creative and affirmative. Sexuality as a life-affirming shaper of community can only be effective when partners accept the responsibilities of caring for one another's happiness.

D. The relationship between women and men should be characterized not by patronizing behavior or exploitation, but by love, partnership, and trustworthiness. Human fulfillment is not identical with sexual pleasure. Sexuality should express and reinforce a loving relationship lived by equal partners. Some religious traditions know the ideal of a voluntary renunciation of the full use of sexuality. Voluntary renunciation also can be an expression of identity and meaningful fulfillment.

E. The social institution of marriage, despite all its cultural and religious variety, is characterized by love, loyalty, and permanence. It aims at and should guarantee security and mutual support to husband, wife, and child. It should secure the rights of all family members. All lands and cultures should develop economic and social relationships which will enable marriage and family life worthy of human beings, especially for older people. Children have a right of access to education. Parents should not exploit children, nor children parents. Their relationships should reflect mutual respect, appreciation, and concern.

F. To be authentically human in the spirit of our great religious and ethical traditions means the following:
   - We need mutual respect, partnership, and understanding, instead of patriarchal domination and degradation, which are expressions of violence and engender counterviolence.
   - We need mutual concern, tolerance, readiness for reconciliation, and love, instead of any form of possessive lust or sexual misuse.

Only what has already been experienced in personal and familial relationships can be practiced on the level of nations and religions.

IV. A Transformation of Consciousness

Historical experience demonstrates the following: Earth cannot be changed for the better unless we achieve a transformation in the consciousness of individuals and in public life. The possibilities for transformation have already been glimpsed in areas such as war and peace, economy, and ecology, where in recent decades fundamental changes have taken place. This transformation must also be achieved in the area of ethics and values! Every individual has intrinsic dignity and inalienable rights, and each also has an inescapable responsibility for what she or he does and does not do. All our decisions and deeds, even our omissions and failures, have consequences.

Keeping this sense of responsibility alive, deepening it and passing it on to future generations, is the special task of religions. We are realistic about what we have achieved in this consensus, and so we urge that the following be observed:

1. A universal consensus on many disputed ethical questions (from bio- and sexual ethics through mass media and scientific ethics to economic and political ethics) will be difficult to attain. Nevertheless, even for many controversial questions, suitable solutions should be attainable in the spirit of the fundamental principles we have jointly developed here.

2. In many areas of life a new consciousness of ethical respon- sibility has already arisen. Therefore we would be pleased if as many professions as possible, such as those of physicians, scientists, business people, journalists, and politicians, would develop up-to-date codes of ethics which would provide specific guidelines for the vexing questions of these partic- ular professions.

3. Above all, we urge the various communities of faith to for- mulate their very specific ethics: What does each faith tra- dition have to say, for example, about the meaning of life and death, the enduring of suffering and the forgiveness of guilt, about selfless sacrifice and the necessity of renuncia- tion, about compassion and joy? These will deepen, and make more specific, the already discernible global ethic.

In conclusion, we appeal to all the inhabitants of this planet. Earth cannot be changed for the better unless the consciousness of indi- viduals is changed. We pledge to work for such transformation in individual and collective consciousness, for the awakening of our spiritual powers through reflection, meditation, prayer, or positive thinking, for a conversion of the heart. Together we can move mountains! Without a willingness to take risks and a readiness to sacrifice there can be no fundamental change in our situation! Therefore we commit ourselves to a common global ethic, to bet- ter mutual understanding, as well as to socially beneficial, peace- fostering, and Earth-friendly ways of life.

We invite all men and women, whether religious or not, to do the same!

There is additional information about the Global Ethic Project on the Internet at www.weltethos.org. *The text of the Declaration is published in English in* Declaration toward a Global Ethic: The Declaration of the Parliament of the World's Religions, *ed. Hans Küng and Karl-Josef Kuschel (London: SCM Press, 1993).*

GLOSSARY

Codex Hammurabi: One of the first written codes of law, decreed by the sixth Babylonian king Hammurabi (reigned 1795–1750 BCE).

Decalogue: A term first used by the Church Fathers for the Ten Commandments given by God to Moses on Mt. Sinai (Exodus 20:2–17 and Deuteronomy 5:6–18).

Feast of Tabernacles: Also know as Sukkot (Hebrew: "booth," "hut"), one of three pilgrimage festivals of biblical origin. During the festival, which lasts for seven days, huts are constructed and Jewish families spend time in the sukkah to be reminded of the years in the wilderness during the Exodus from Egypt.

Halakhah: Individual rule as well as a general term for all of Jewish religious law.

Hashem: (Hebrew: "God" or "the Name") A word used to refer to God by many people of the Jewish faith.

Haskalah: (Hebrew: "enlightenment") Originated among German Jewry during the late eighteenth century, a European movement cherishing the values of enlightenment, fostering the acquisition of secular knowledge, and raising interest in Hebrew and Jewish historical research.

Karaites: Jewish sect that arose in the eighth century and spread in the tenth and eleventh centuries among Jews in Asia and Europe. In their religious observances, the Karaites strictly follow the Tanakh and disregard later developments such as the Mishnah and Talmud.

Midrash: (Hebrew: "to investigate," "to study") A term that can refer to the act of comparative exegesis of biblical texts or can identify whole compilations of commentaries on the Tanakh (midrashim).

Mishnah: (Hebrew: "repetition") A compilation of Jewish oral law, collected by rabbinic sages during the first and second centuries; the basis for the Talmud.

Mishneh Torah: A code of Jewish religious law, compiled by Moses Maimonides between 1170 and 1180.

Mitzvah: (Hebrew: "commandment," pl., "mitzvot") Describes any activity of human kindness; the plural summarizes all obligations of the Jewish law.

Monotheism: The worship and acceptance of just one God.

Pharisaism: Derived from the Pharisees, a Jewish religious, political, and social movement within the time of the Second Temple, and the basis for rabbinic Judaism.

Polytheism: The adoration of a multitude of gods.

Septuagint: (Latin: *septuaginta interpretum versio*, "translation of the seventy interpreters") Oldest translation of the Tanakh into Greek language, compiled by Jewish scholars in Alexandria from the third to the first century BCE.

Shechinah: God's presence in the world.

Shemoneh Esrei: The central prayer in Jewish liturgy composed of nineteen blessings.

Talmud: Compendium of rabbinic discussions pertaining to Jewish law, stories, customs, and history. The Talmud exists in two different versions, the *Talmud Yerushalmi* (Jerusalem Talmud) and the *Talmud Bavli* (Babylonian Talmud), in the ancient centers of Jewish scholarship, the Land of Israel and Babylonia, and both were compiled during the fourth through sixth centuries CE.

Tanakh: Holy scripture used in Judaism. The Tanakh consists of three divisions: Torah, *Nevi'im* ("Prophets"), and *Ketuvim* ("Writings"); its name "TaNaKh" is an acronym formed from their initial Hebrew letters. Although the compilation of the Torah is said to have ended around 400 BCE, the final canonization process of the Tanakh was completed about 100 CE.

Tefillah: Prayer.

Theodicy: Classical philosophical and theological problem reconciling the existence of evil and suffering in the world with the existence of an almighty, all-knowing, and gracious God.

Tikkun Olam: The healing of the world.

Torah: (Hebrew: "learning," "instruction") First main division of the Tanakh and composed of five books (*Bereshit* = Genesis, *Shemot* = Exodus, *Vayikra* = Leviticus, *Bemidbar* = Numbers, and *Devarim* = Deuteronomy), hence also designated as Pentateuch or Five Books of Moses. The latter refers to the authorship of Moses according to the Jewish religious tradition.

Tzedakah: Religious obligation for Jews to practice charity, and above all to exercise social justice.

YHVH: The biblical name for God used by the ancient Hebrews.

SOURCES

Texts from the Tanakh are cited according to:

Tanakh: A New Translation of the Holy Scriptures According to the Traditional Hebrew Text. Philadelphia: Jewish Publication Society, 1985.

Apocrypha and Pseudepigrapha (early Jewish literature that was not incorporated into the rabbinic canon of the Tanakh) are cited according to:

The Apocrypha and Pseudepigrapha of the Old Testament in English. Edited in conjunction with many scholars by R. H. Charles. London: Oxford University Press, 1973.

Texts from the Babylonian Talmud are cited according to:

The Babylonian Talmud. Translated into English with notes, glossary, and indices under the editorship of I. Epstein. London: Soncino Press, 1978.

NOTES

INTRODUCTION

1. Von Eberhard von Gemmingen, "Unsere Anliegen decken sich jetzt," *Die Welt* (October 10, 2005), http://www.welt.de/print welt/article168652/Unsere_Anliegen_decken_sich_jetzt.html.
2. Vatican, "Address of His Holiness Benedict XVI," 2008, http://www.vatican.va/holy_father/benedict_xvi/speeches/2008/april/documents/hf_ben-xvi_spe_20080417_other-religions_en.html.

JUDAISM'S UNIVERSAL GIFT

1. Jakob J. Petuchowski, *New Perspectives on Abraham Geiger* (Cincinnati: Hebrew Union College–Jewish Institute of Religion, 1975). Caption on the portrait of Abraham Geiger taken between 1840 and 1843 in Breslau. The portrait is in the American Jewish Archives, Cincinnati.
2. Hermann Cohen, *Religion of Reason: Out of the Sources of Judaism*, translated, with an introduction by Simon Kaplan (Atlanta: Scholars Press, 1995), 84.
3. David Novak, "Hermann Cohen and Noachidic Law," in Helmut Holzhey, Gabriel Matzkin, and Hartwig Wiedebach, eds., *Religion der Vernunft aus den Quellen des Judentums: Tradition und Ursprungsdenken in Hermann Cohen's Spätwerk* (Zurich and New York: Georg Olms, 2000), 226.
4. Jonathan A. Romain and Walter Homolka, *Progressive Judaism: Law and Lore* (Munich: Knesebeck, 1999), 20.
5. BT, *Avodah Zarah* 44b, 54b–55a; BT, *Sanhedrin* 91ab. Aharon Shear-Yashuv, "Der universale Aspekt des Judentums: Israel und die Völkerwelt," in *Religion, Philosophy and Judaism* (Jerusalem: Yair Giat, 1987), 232–240.
6. *Pirke Avot* 5:25; BT, *Megillah* 19b.
7. BT, *Menachot* 29b.
8. BT, *Bava Metzia* 59ab.
9. BT, *Eruvin* 13b.
10. Romain and Homolka, *Progressive Judaism*, 23.

11. Abraham J. Heschel, *God in Search of Man: Philosophy of Judaism* (Neukirchen-Vluyn: Neukirchener Verlag, 1980), 218.

12. *Pirke Avot* 3:14.

13. Ben Sirakh 17:3, 6–7.

14. Ben Sirakh 15:11–20.

15. Ben Sirakh 39:16.

16. Ben Sirakh 15:14.

17. Midrash Genesis Rabbah (Bereshit Rabbah) 9:7.

18. Ben Sirakh 15:20.

19. *Pirke Avot* 4:1.

20. John D. Rayner, "Good and Evil in the Classical Sources of Judaism," in *Signposts to the Messianic Age* (London: Vallentine Mitchell, 2006), 179.

21. Philo, "Quod omnis probus liber sit" [How far every good man is free], in *Works*, vol. 10, ed. and trans. F. H. Colson (London: Heinemann and Cambridge, Mass.: Harvard University Press, 1941), 3, 21.

22. For the question of the assessment of the natural law by the Rabbis, cf. David S. Shapiro, "The Doctrine of the Image of God and Imitatio Dei"; Martin Bucher, "Imitatio Dei"; Chaim W. Reines, "The Self and the Other in Rabbinic Ethics"; against: Aharon Lichtenstein, "Does Jewish Tradition Recognize an Ethic Independent of Halakhah?" All the articles are in Menachem Marc Kellner, ed., *Contemporary Jewish Ethics* (New York: Sanhedrin Press, 1978).

23. Already in Ben Sirakh (1:1–10) there is a distinction between knowledge bestowed on all human beings and knowledge specially bestowed only on Israel. The wisdom accessible to all human beings consists in the fact that God gives them a share of the wisdom with which God made heaven and earth. Cf. Otto Kaiser, *Human Happiness and God's Righteousness: Biblical Tradition in the Context of Hellenistic Philosophy* (Tübingen: J. C. B. Mohr [Paul Siebeck], 2007).

24. Kaufmann Kohler, *Jewish Theology: Systematically and Historically Considered* (Leipzig: Buchhandlung Gustav Fock, 1910), 242–243.

25. Hermann Cohen, *Religion of Reason* (n. 2), 116–117. Cf. Christoph Schulte, "Noachidische Gebote und Naturrecht," in Holzhey, Matzkin, and Wiedebach, *Religion der Vernunft aus den Quellen des Judentums* (n. 3), 248.

26. Novak, "Das noachidische Naturrecht" (n. 3), 233.

27. Cf. BT, *Chullin* 13a on the question whether the sacrifice would be accepted by non-Jews.

28. "Now only Balaam will not enter [the future world], but other [heathen] will enter. On whose authority is the Mishnah [taught]?—On R. Joshua's" (BT, *Sanhedrin* 105a).

29. *Mishneh Torah, Melachim* 8, 11. Cf. Hermann Cohen, "Charity in Talmud" (1888), in Bruno Strauss, ed., *Jüdische Schriften*, vol. 1 (Berlin: Schwetschke, 1924), 145–174.

30. *Mishneh Torah, Melachim* 10, 7.

31. Flavius Josephus, *Jewish Antiquities* 20, 2, 4, 17–45.

32. Cf. Walter Homolka and Esther Seidel eds., *Nicht durch Geburt allein: Übertritt zum Judentum* (Berlin: Frank & Timme, 2006).

33. Flusser, "Noachidic Laws Part One " (n. 34); Klaus Müller, *Tora für die Völker: Die noachidischen Gebote und Ansätze zu ihrer Rezeption im Christentum* (Berlin and New York: De Gruyter, 1994); Aaron Lichtenstein, *The Seven Laws of Noah* (New York: Rabbi Jacob Joseph Press, 1981); Chaim Clorfene and Yakov Rogalsky, *The Path of the Righteous Gentile: An Introduction to the Seven Laws of the Children of Noah* (New York: Targum Press, 1987).

34. Moses Mendelssohn, *Collected Works*, ed. Simon Rawidowicz, vol. 7 (Berlin: Akademie Verlag, 1930), 14 and 10. For the history of the reception of the Noachide commandments in Judaism, cf. Schulte, "Noachidische Gebote und Naturrecht" (n. 25), 245–274.

35. BT, *Bava Kama* 38a.

36. Cf. BT, *Avodah Zarah* 64b; BT, *Chullin* 92a–b.

37. BT, *Sanhedrin* 74 b. Idolatry, adultery, and the shedding of blood are the oldest basic elements. In the first half of the first century CE, theft and blasphemy were also added. The list of seven commandments and prohibitions is attested at the latest from the second half of the second century CE. Cf. David Flusser, "Noachidic Laws Part One," in *Theologische Realenzyklopädie*, vol. 24 (Berlin and New York: De Gruyter, 1994), 582–585.

38. Midrash Deuteronomy Rabbah (Devarim Rabbah) 2:25 on Deuteronomy 4:41.

39. Moses Maimonides, *Mishneh Torah, Melachim* 9, 1.

40. Hermann Cohen, *Religion of Reason* (n. 2), 122–123.

CORE ETHIC 1 The Value of the Human: Every human being must be treated humanely.

1. Abraham J. Heschel (1907–1972), "Sacred Image of Man," in *The Insecurity of Freedom* (New York: Farrar, Straus & Giroux, 1967), 150–156.

2. Samson Hochfeld (1872–1921), "Human Equity," in *The Teaching of Judaism According to the Sources*, new edition by Walter Homolka, vol. 1 (Munich: Knesebeck, 1999), 98–99. Translation by John Bowden.

3. *Philo*, with an English translation by F. H. Colson, vol. 7 (London: Heinemann and Cambridge, Mass.: Harvard University Press, 1958), 26–27.
4. Ibid., 527.
5. Herbert Danby, *The Mishnah*, translated from the Hebrew with an introduction and brief explanatory notes (London: Oxford University Press, 1933), 388.
6. Ibid.
7. *The Midrash on Psalms*, vol. 2, translation by William G. Braude (New Haven: Yale University Press, 1959), 243.
8. Jacob Neusner, *Sifra: An Analytical Translation*, vol. 3 (Atlanta, Ga: Scholars Press, 1988), 80.
9. Moses Hayyim Luzzatto (1707–1746), *Mesillat Yesharim* (The Path of the Upright), a critical edition provided with a translation and notes by Mordecai M. Kaplan (Philadelphia: The Jewish Publication Society of America, 1948), 148.
10. Baal Shem Tov (1700–1760), in B. Z. Barslai, *Rabbinic Wisdom* (Gütersloh: Gütersloher Verlagshaus, 1993), 27. Translation by John Bowden.
11. W. Gunther Plaut et al., eds., *The Torah: A Modern Commentary*, rev. ed., (New York: URJ Press, 2006), 1220.
12. Abraham Geiger (1810–1874), *Judaism and Its History*, translated from the German by Maurice Mayer (New York: M. Thalmessinger and London: Trübner, 1865), 75. Kessinger Publishing Reprints, www.kessinger.net.
13. Samson Raphael Hirsch (1808–1888), *Horeb: A Philosophy of Jewish Laws and Observances*, translated from the German original with introduction and annotations by Dayan Dr. I. Grunfeld (New York, London, and Jerusalem: The Soncino Press, 2002), 255–256.
14. Heymann Steinthal (1823–1899), *Lectures and Writings on Bible and Philosophy of Religion*, vol. 1 (Berlin: G. Reimer, 1895), 178–179. Translation by John Bowden.
15. Moritz Güdemann (1835–1918), *Teaching and History: A Basic Frame of Judaism* (Vienna: Löwit, 1902), 36. Translation by John Bowden.
16. Hermann Cohen (1842–1918), *Religion of Reason, Out of the Sources of Judaism*, translated, with an introduction by Simon Kaplan (Atlanta, Ga: Scholars Press, 1995), 120–121.
17. Kaufmann Kohler (1843–1926), *Jewish Theology, Systematically and Historically Considered* (New York: Ktav, 1968), 122.
18. Simon Dubnow (1860–1941), *Schto takoje Jewreskaja istorija*, German by Israel Friedländer, *Die Jüdische Geschichte* (Berlin: Calvary, 1898),

25f. There is an English translation, *Jewish History—An Essay in the Philosophy of History* (Philadelphia: Jewish Publication Society, 1903), but this was not accessible to us. Translation by John Bowden.

19. Leo Baeck (1873–1956), *The Essence of Judaism* (New York: Schocken Books, 1948), 152.

20. Ibid., 191.

21. Ibid., 70.

22. Martin Buber (1878–1965), *I and Thou*, a new translation with a prologue "I and Thou" and notes by Walter Kaufmann (New York: Charles Scribner's Sons, 1970), 59–60.

CORE ETHIC 2   The Golden Rule: Do not do to another what you would not want to be done to you.

1. Samson Hochfeld (1872–1921), "Human Charity," in *The Teaching of Judaism According to the Sources*, new edition by Walter Homolka, vol. 1 (Munich: Knesebeck, 1999), 328–331.

2. Franz Rosenzweig (1886–1929), *The Star of Redemption*, translated from the second edition of 1930 by William W. Hallo (Notre Dame: University of Notre Dame Press, 1985), 218, 239–240, 259.

3. C. G. Montefiore and H. Loewe, *A Rabbinic Anthology* (London: Macmillan, 1938), 172–173.

4. *The Fathers According to Rabbi Nathan*, translated from the Hebrew by Judah Goldin (New Haven and London: Yale University Press, 1955), 82.

5. Bachya ben Joseph ibn Paquda (eleventh century), *Duties of the Heart*, translated from the Arabic into Hebrew by Jehuda ibn Tibbon, with English translation by Moses Hyamson, vol. 2 (Jerusalem: Boys Town Jerusalem Publishers, 1965), 251.

6. Rabbi Shlomo ben Yizhak (1040–1105), in *Seder ha-Tefillot* (*The Jewish Prayerbook*), edited by Jonathan Magonet in collaboration with Walter Homolka, vol. 2 (Gütersloh: Gütersloher Verlagshaus, 1997), 18. Translation by John Bowden.

7. Moses ibn Ezra (eleventh/twelfth century), in Salcia Landmann, *3,000 Years of Jewish Wisdom* (Munich and Berlin: Droemer Knaur, 1983), 170. Translation by John Bowden.

8. Moses Maimonides (1138–1204), *Mishneh Torah: The Book of Knowledge*, edited according to the Bodleian (Oxford) Codex with introduction, biblical and Talmudical references, notes, and English translation by Moses Hyamson (Jerusalem and New York: Feldheim Publishers, 1981), 86b–87a.

9. Ibid., 55a.
10. Jacob ben Abbamari (1194–1215), *Malmad ha-Talmidim* 72b, quoted from *The Teaching of Judaism According to the Sources*, new edition by Walter Homolka, vol. 1 (Munich: Knesebeck, 1999), 189. Translation by John Bowden.
11. Yehudah HeChasid (1140–1217), *Sefer Chassidim: The Book of the Pious*, condensed, translated, and annotated by Avraham Yaakov Finkel (Northvale, N.J. and London: Jason Aronson, 1997), 108–109.
12. Joseph Albo (1380–1444), *Sefer Ha-'Ikkarim: Book of Principles*, critically edited on the basis of manuscripts and old editions and provided with a translation and notes by Isaac Husik (Philadelphia: The Jewish Publication Society of America, 1930), 237.
13. Moses Hayyim Luzzatto (1707–1746), *Mesillat Yesharim: The Path of the Upright*, a critical edition provided with a translation and notes by Mordecai M. Kaplan (Philadelphia: The Jewish Publication Society of America, 1948), 90.
14. Baal Shem Tov (1700–1760), in *Seder ha-Tefillot (Rabbinic Wisdom)*, edited by Jonathan Magonet in collaboration with Walter Homolka, vol. 2 (Gütersloh: Gütersloher Verlagshaus, 1997),18. Translation by John Bowden.
15. Jaakob Jossef from Polonia, quoted from Benyamin Z. Barslai, *Rabbinic Wisdom* (Gütersloh: Gütersloher Verlagshaus, 1993), 25. Translation by John Bowden.
16. Abraham Geiger (1810–1874), *Judaism and Its History*, translated from the German by Maurice Mayer (New York: M. Thalmessinger and London: Trübner, 1865), 73. Kessinger Publishing Reprints www.kessinger.net.
17. Samson Raphael Hirsch (1808–1888), *Horeb: A Philosophy of Jewish Laws and Observances*, translated from the German original with introduction and annotations by Dayan Dr. I. Grunfeld (New York, London, and Jerusalem: The Soncino Press, 2002), 52–53.
18. Heymann Steinthal (1823–1899), *Jews and Judaism* (Berlin: M. Poppelauer, 1906), 117–118. Translation by John Bowden.
19. Moritz Lazarus (1824–1903), *The Ethics of Judaism*, Part 2 (Philadelphia: The Jewish Publication Society of America, 1901), 60–61.
20. Moses Bloch (1815–1909), *Ethics in Halakha* (Budapest: Athenaeum, 1886), 9. Translation by John Bowden.
21. Franz Rosenzweig, *The Star of Redemption* (n. 1), 214.
22. Max Wiener (1882–1950), *The Religion of the Prophets* (Frankfurt am Main: Kauffmann, 1912), 11–12. Translation by John Bowden.

23. Leo Baeck (1873–1956), *The Essence of Judaism* (New York: Schocken Books, 1948), 35–36.
24. Ibid., 213–214.
25. Louis Jacobs (1920–2006), *Jewish Personal and Social Ethics* (West Orange, N.J.: Behrman House, 1990), 55–57.

CORE ETHIC 3   Peace: Commitment to a culture of nonviolence and reverence for all life.

1. Hermann Cohen (1842–1918), *Religion of Reason, Out of the Sources of Judaism*, translated, with an introduction by Simon Kaplan (Atlanta, Ga: Scholars Press, 1995), 451–454.
2. Leo Baeck (1873–1956), *The Essence of Judaism* (New York: Schocken Books, 1948), 215–216.
3. *Philo*, with an English translation by F. H. Colson, vol. 8 (London: Heinemann and Cambridge, Mass.: Harvard University Press, 1960), 229.
4. Flavius Josephus (died 100), *Against Apion* II, 29, in Flavius Josephus, *The Life: Against Apion*, with an English translation by H. St. J. Thackeray (Cambridge, Mass., and London: Harvard University Press, 1993 [reprinted]), 379.
5. *The Talmud of the Land of Israel*, vol. 1, *Berakhot* (Chicago and London: University of Chicago Press, 1989), 168–169.
6. *Midrash Rabbah*, ed. H. Freedman and Maurice Simon, *Numbers II* (London: Soncino Press, 1939), 777.
7. Midrash Deuteronomy Rabbah (Devarim Rabbah) 5: 12, from E. Goldberg, *Swords and Plowshares* (New York: URJ Press, 2006) 99.
8. *Midrash Rabbah*, ed. H. Freedman and Maurice Simon, vol. 7, *Deuteronomy* (London: Soncino Press, 1939), 117–118.
9. *Midrash Rabbah*, ed. H. Freedman and Maurice Simon, vol. 8, *Ruth and Ecclesiastes* (London: Soncino Press, 1939), 195–196.
10. Hayim Nahman Bialik and Yehoshua Hana Ravnitzky, eds., *The Book of Legends: Sefer Ha-Aggadah; Legends from the Talmud and Midrash* (New York: Schocken Books, 1992), 690.
11. Saadya Fayyumi (Saadya Gaon) (882–942), *Theology and Philiosophy* 3, 5 (Hildesheim: Georg Olms, 1970), 198–199. Translation by John Bowden.
12. Moses Maimonides (1135–1204), *The Code of Maimonides: Book Fourteen, The Book of Judges*, translated from the Hebrew by Abraham M. Hershman (New Haven and London: Yale University Press, 1977), 240–242.

13. Isaac Ben Solomon Luria (Ha-Ari) (1534–1572), in W. Gunther Plaut et al., eds., *The Torah: A Modern Commentary*, rev. ed. (New York: URJ Press, 2006), 1220.
14. Baal Shem Tov (1700–1760), in B. Z. Barslai, *Rabbinic Wisdom* (Gütersloh: Gütersloher Verlagshaus, 1993), 21. Translation by John Bowden.
15. Samson Raphael Hirsch (1808–1888), *Horeb: A Philosophy of Jewish Laws and Observances*, translated from the German original with introduction and annotations by Dayan Dr. I. Grunfeld (New York, London, and Jerusalem: The Soncino Press, 2002), 223.
16. Moritz Lazarus (1824–1903), *The Ethics of Judaism*, translated from the German by Henrietta Szold, Part 2 (Philadelphia: Jewish Publication Society of America, 1901), 249–50.
17. Franz Rosenzweig (1886–1929), *The Star of Redemption*, translated from the second edition of 1930 by William W. Hallo (Notre Dame: University of Notre Dame Press, 1985), 330–331.
18. H. G. Brandt, ed., *Or Chadasch: Gebete für Schabbat, Fest- und Wochentage* (Zurich, 1981), 124. Translation by John Bowden.

CORE ETHIC 4 Justice: Commitment to a culture of justice and a just economic order.

1. Salomo Samuel (1867–1942), V., "Public Welfare," in *The Teaching of Judaism According to the Sources*, new edition by Walter Homolka, vol. 2 (Munich: Knesebeck, 1999), 112–114. Translation by John Bowden.
2. Leo Baeck (1873–1956), "Judaism and Its Social Character," in ibid., 9–11. Translation by John Bowden.
3. *Philo*, with an English translation by F. H. Colson, vol. 7 (London: Heinemann and Cambridge, Mass.: Harvard University Press, 1958), 347.
4. Flavius Josephus (died 100), *Jewish Antiquities: Books I–IV*, with an English translation by H. St. J. Thackeray (London and Cambridge, Mass.: Harvard University Press, 1991), 589.
5. *The Midrash on Psalms*, translated from the Hebrew and Aramaic by William G. Braude (New Haven: Yale University Press, 1959), 368.
6. *Seder Eliyahu Rabbah* (tenth century), quoted from Walter Homolka, ed., "So gehe ich meinen Weg mit Gott," in *Jewish Prayers* (Gütersloh: Gütersloher Verlagshaus, 2000), 68. Translation by John Bowden.
7. Ibid., 69.
8. Moses Maimonides (1138–1204), *Mishneh Torah: The Book of Knowledge*, edited according to the Bodleian (Oxford) Codex with

introduction, biblical and Talmudical references, notes, and English translation by Moses Hyamson (Jerusalem and New York: Feldheim, 1981), 91–92.

9. Moses Hayyim Luzzatto (1707–1746), *Mesillat Yesharim: The Path of the Upright*, a critical edition provided with a translation and notes by Mordecai M. Kaplan (Philadelphia: The Jewish Publication Society of America, 1948), 76–77.

10. Menachem Mendel of Kozk (died 1859), in *Seder ha-Tefillot: Das Jüdische Gebetsbuch*, edited by Jonathan Magonet in collaboration with Walter Homolka, vol. 1 (Gütersloh: Gütersloher Verlagshaus, 1997), 74. Translation by John Bowden.

11. Solomon Ganzfried (1804–1886), *Code of Jewish Law: Kitzur Shulchan Arukh; A Compilation of Jewish Laws and Customs*, vol. 2, translated by Hyman E. Goldin (New York: Hebrew Publishing Company, 1963), 36.

12. Moses Bloch (1815–1909), *Ethics in Halakha* (Budapest: Athenaeum, 1886), 54f. Translation by John Bowden.

13. Hermann Cohen (1842–1918), *Religion of Reason, Out of the Sources of Judaism*, translated, with an introduction by Simon Kaplan (Atlanta, Ga: Scholars Press, 1995), 430–431.

14. Ibid., 143.

15. Max Wiener (1882–1950), *The Religion of the Prophets* (Frankfurt am Main: Kauffmann, 1912), 75f. Translation by John Bowden.

16. Simon Bernfeld (1860–1940), "Human Equity," in *The Teaching of Judaism According to the Sources* (Munich: Knesebeck, 1999), 20. Translation by John Bowden.

17. Haim Cohn (1911–2002), *Human Rights in Jewish Law* (New York: Ktav, 1984), 189.

CORE ETHIC 5 Truth and Tolerance: Commitment to a culture of tolerance and a life in truthfulness.

1. Leo Baeck (1873–1956), "Truthfulness," in *The Teachings of Judaism According to the Sources*, new edition by Walter Homolka, vol. 1 (Munich: Knesebeck, 1999), 151–153. Translation by John Bowden.

2. Moses Maimonides (1138–1204), *Mishneh Torah: The Book of Knowledge*, edited according to the Bodleian (Oxford) Codex with introduction, biblical and Talmudical references, notes, and English translation by Moses Hyamson (Jerusalem and New York: Feldheim, 1981), 92a–92b.

3. R. H. Charles, *The Apocrypha and Pseudepigrapha of the Old Testament*, vol. 1 (London: Oxford University Press, 1973), 32.
4. Herbert Danby, *The Mishnah*, translated from the Hebrew with an introduction and brief explanatory notes (London: Oxford University Press, 1933), 387–88.
5. *The Talmud of the Land of Israel*, vol. 8, *Taanit* (Atlanta, Ga: Scholars Press, 1998), 92.
6. Hayim Nahman Bialik and Yehoshua Hana Ravnitzky, eds., *The Book of Legends: Sefer Ha-Aggadah; Legends from the Talmud and Midrash* (New York: Schocken Books, 1992), 696.
7. Salomo ben Mose from Rome (Middle Ages), quoted from Moritz Güdemann, *History of Jewish Education and Culture in Medieval Italy*, vol. 2 (Amsterdam: Philo Press, 1966), 232. Translation by John Bowden.
8. Moses Maimonides (1138–1204), *Mishneh Torah* (n. 2), 49a.
9. Moses Maimonides (1138–1204), *Commentary on Pirke Avot* 1:17, from Gilbert S. Rosenthal, ed., *Maimonides: His Wisdom for Our Time* (New York: Funk & Wagnalls, 1969), 19f.
10. Solomon Ganzfried (1804–1886), *Code of Jewish Law: Kitzur Shulhan Arukh; A Compilation of Jewish Laws and Customs*, vol. 4, translated by Hyman E. Goldin (New York: Hebrew Publishing Company, 1963), 69.
11. Moses Hayyim Luzzatto (1707–1746), *Mesillat Yesharim: The Path of the Upright*, a critical edition provided with a translation and notes by Mordecai M. Kaplan (Philadelphia: The Jewish Publication Society of America, 1948), 87–89.
12. Ibid., 91.
13. Rabbi Nachman of Breslov (1772–1810), in B. Z. Barslai, *Rabbinic Wisdom* (Gütersloh: Gütersloher Verlagshaus, 1993), 24. Translation by John Bowden.
14. Samson Raphael Hirsch (1808–1888), *Horeb: A Philosophy of Jewish Laws and Observances*, translated from the German original with introduction and annotations by Dayan Dr. I. Grunfeld (New York, London, and Jerusalem: The Soncino Press, 2002), 250, 252.
15. Hermann Cohen (1842–1918), *Religion of Reason: Out of the Sources of Judaism*, translated with an introduction by Simon Kaplan (Atlanta, Ga: Scholars Press, 1995), 421–423.
16. Martin Buber, "The Way of Man, According to the Teachings of Chassidism, in *Martin Buber, Hasidism and Modern Man*, edited and translated by Maurice Freeman (New York: Horizon Press, 1958), 158.

CORE ETHIC 6 Equal Rights: Commitment to a culture of equal rights and a partnership between men and women.

1. Judith Plaskow (born 1946), *Standing Again at Sinai: Judaism from a Feminist Perspective* (San Francisco: Harper & Row, 1990), 87–90.
2. Moses Maimonides (1138–1204), *Mishneh Torah: Book Four, The Book of Women*, translated from the Hebrew by Isaac Klein (New Haven and London: Yale University Press, 1972), 73–74.
3. *Philo*, with an English translation by F. H. Colson, vol. 7 (London: Heinemann and Cambridge, Mass.: Harvard University Press, 1958), 121.
4. C. G. Montefiore and H. Loewe, *A Rabbinic Anthology* (London: Macmillan, 1938), 510.
5. Ibid., 537.
6. Genesis Rabbah 8:9 and 22:2, in *Midrash Rabbah*, ed. H. Freedman and Maurice Simon, *Genesis I* (London: Soncino Press, 1939), 61, 181.
7. Montefiore and Loewe, *A Rabbinic Anthology* (n. 4), 511.
8. Hayim Nahman Bialik and Yehoshua Hana Ravnitzky, eds., *The Book of Legends: Sefer Ha-Aggadah; Legends from the Talmud and Midrash* (New York: Schocken Books, 1992), 616.
9. Ibid., 167.
10. Ibid., 627–628.
11. Maimonides (1138–1204), *Mishneh Torah: Book Four, The Book of Women* (n. 2), IV, 1, 22.
12. Ibid., XII, 4, 74.
13. Ibid., XIV, 8, 89.
14. Yehudah HeChasid (1140–1217), *Sefer Chassidim: The Book of the Pious*, condensed, translated, and annotated by Avraham Yaakov Finkel (Northvale, N.J. and London: Jason Aronson, 1997), 321.
15. Glikl bas Judah Leib, also "Glückel of Hamelin" (1646–1724), from the memoirs of Glückel of Hamelin, quoted in E. Tannenbaum and E. Fraenkel, *Philo Encyclopedia of Quotations: Words of Jews for Jews* (Berlin: Philo, 1936), 149. Translation by John Bowden.
16. Abraham Geiger (1810–1874), *Judaism and Its History*, translated from the German by Maurice Mayer (New York: M. Thalmessinger and London: Trübner, 1865), 78. Kessinger Publishing Reprints www.kessinger.net.
17. Samson Raphael Hirsch (1808–1888), *Horeb: A Philosophy of Jewish Laws and Observances*, translated from the German original with introduction and annotations by Dayan Dr. I. Grunfeld (New York, London, and Jerusalem: The Soncino Press, 2002), 401.

18. Hermann Cohen (1842–1918), *Religion of Reason: Out of the Sources of Judaism*, translated, with an introduction by Simon Kaplan (Atlanta, Ga: Scholars Press, 1995), 442–443.
19. Menachem Mendel Schneerson, *A Woman's Place in Torah: Sichos in English* (New York, 1990), http://www.chabad.org/theJewishWoman/article_cdo/aid/395067/jewish/A-Womans-Place-in-Torah.htm.
20. Rachel Adler, "Engendering Judaism," in *Contemporary Jewish Theology: A Reader*, edited by Elliot N. Dorff and Louis E. Newman (New York and Oxford: Oxford University Press, 1999), 322–323.
21. Retold from the Yiddish; see Immanuel Olsvanger, *Rosinkess mit Mandlen: Schwänke, Erzählungen, Sprichwörter, Rätsel; Aus der Volksliteratur der Ostjuden* (Zürich: Arche, 1965), 259. Translation by John Bowden.

AFTERWORD A Vision of Hope: Religious Peace and a Global Ethic

1. Hans Küng, *Global Responsibility* (London: SCM Press and New York: Crossroad, 1991).
2. Cf. Hans Küng and Karl-Josef Kuschel, eds., *Declaration toward a Global Ethic: The Declaration of the Parliament of the World's Religions* (London, 1993). Cf. www.weltethos.org.
3. Hans Küng, *A Global Ethic for Global Politics and Global Economics*, (London: SCM Press and New York: Continuum, 1997).
4. InterAction Council, "World Religions as a Factor in World Politics" (Tübingen, Germany, May 7–8, 2007).

CREDITS

Rachel Adler, [excerpt from:] "Engendering Judaism," in *Contemporary Jewish Theology. A Reader*. Edited by Elliot N. Dorff and Louis E. Newman, New York and Oxford © 1990 The Jewish Publication Society, Philadelphia PA, USA.

Leo Baeck, [excerpts from:] Leo Baeck, *The Essence of Judaism*, New York © 1948 Schocken Books, with permission by Random House Inc., New York, NY, USA.

Hayim Nahman Bialik, Yehoshua Hana Ravnitzky, [excerpts from:] *The Book of Legends. Sefer Ha-Aggadah. Legends from the Talmud and Midrash*, New York © 1992 Schocken Books, with permission by Random House Inc., New York, NY, USA.

Martin Buber, [excerpt from:] *I and Thou*. A new translation with a prologue "I and Thou" and notes by Walter Kaufmann, New York © 1970 Charles Scribner's Sons, with permission by Simon & Schuster Inc., New York, NY, USA.

Haim Cohn, [excerpt from:] *Human Rights in Jewish Law*, New York 1984 © Michal Smoira Cohn, Tel Aviv, Israel.

Edwin S. Goldberg, [excerpt from:] *Swords and Plowshares*, New York © 2006 URJ Books & Music, New York, NY, USA.

Abraham Joshua Heschel, [excerpt from:] "Sacred Image of Man," in *The Insecurity of Freedom*, New York © 1967 Farrar, Straus & Giroux, with permission by Macmillian, New York, NY, USA.

Louis Jacobs, [excerpt from:] *Jewish Personal & Social Ethics* © 1990 Behrman House, Inc., Springfield, NJ, USA.

Jacob Neusner, [excerpts from:] *The Talmud of the Land of Israel*, Chicago and London © 1989 The University of Chicago Press, Chicago, IL, USA.

Judith Plaskow, [excerpt from:] *Standing Again at Sinai. Judaism from a Feminist Perspective*, San Francisco © 1990 Harper & Row Publishers, with permission by HarperCollins Publishers, New York, NY, USA.

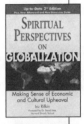
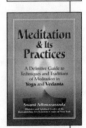

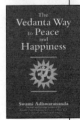

Spiritual Practice

Soul Fire: Accessing Your Creativity *by Rev. Thomas Ryan, CSP*
Shows you how to cultivate your creative spirit as a way to encourage personal growth.
6 x 9, 160 pp, Quality PB, 978-1-59473-243-0 **$16.99**

Running—The Sacred Art: Preparing to Practice
by Dr. Warren A. Kay; Foreword by Kristin Armstrong
Examines how your daily run can enrich your spiritual life.
5½ x 8½, 160 pp, Quality PB, 978-1-59473-227-0 **$16.99**

Hospitality—The Sacred Art: Discovering the Hidden Spiritual Power
of Invitation and Welcome *by Rev. Nanette Sawyer; Foreword by Rev. Dirk Ficca*
Explores how this ancient spiritual practice can transform your relationships.
5½ x 8½, 192 pp, Quality PB, 978-1-59473-228-7 **$16.99**

Thanking & Blessing—The Sacred Art: Spiritual Vitality through
Gratefulness *by Jay Marshall, PhD; Foreword by Philip Gulley*
Offers practical tips for uncovering the blessed wonder in our lives—even in trying circumstances. 5½ x 8½, 176 pp, Quality PB, 978-1-59473-231-7 **$16.99**

Everyday Herbs in Spiritual Life: A Guide to Many Practices
by Michael J. Caduto; Foreword by Rosemary Gladstar Explores the power of herbs.
7 x 9, 208 pp, 21 b/w illustrations, Quality PB, 978-1-59473-174-7 **$16.99**

Divining the Body: Reclaim the Holiness of Your Physical Self *by Jan Phillips*
8 x 8, 256 pp, Quality PB, 978-1-59473-080-1 **$16.99**

Finding Time for the Timeless: Spirituality in the Workweek
by John McQuiston II Simple stories show you how refocus your daily life.
5½ x 6¾, 208 pp, HC, 978-1-59473-035-1 **$17.99**

The Gospel of Thomas: A Guidebook for Spiritual Practice
by Ron Miller; Translations by Stevan Davies
6 x 9, 160 pp, Quality PB, 978-1-59473-047-4 **$14.99**

Earth, Water, Fire, and Air: Essential Ways of Connecting to Spirit
by Cait Johnson 6 x 9, 224 pp, HC, 978-1-893361-65-2 **$19.95**

Labyrinths from the Outside In: Walking to Spiritual Insight—A Beginner's Guide
by Donna Schaper and Carole Ann Camp
6 x 9, 208 pp, b/w illus. and photos, Quality PB, 978-1-893361-18-8 **$16.95**

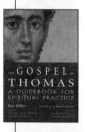

Practicing the Sacred Art of Listening: A Guide to Enrich Your Relationships
and Kindle Your Spiritual Life—The Listening Center Workshop
by Kay Lindahl 8 x 8, 176 pp, Quality PB, 978-1-893361-85-0 **$16.95**

Releasing the Creative Spirit: Unleash the Creativity in Your Life
by Dan Wakefield 7 x 10, 256 pp, Quality PB, 978-1-893361-36-2 **$16.95**

The Sacred Art of Bowing: Preparing to Practice
by Andi Young 5½ x 8½, 128 pp, b/w illus., Quality PB, 978-1-893361-82-9 **$14.95**

The Sacred Art of Chant: Preparing to Practice
by Ana Hernández 5½ x 8½, 192 pp, Quality PB, 978-1-59473-036-8 **$15.99**

The Sacred Art of Fasting: Preparing to Practice
by Thomas Ryan, CSP 5½ x 8½, 192 pp, Quality PB, 978-1-59473-078-8 **$15.99**

The Sacred Art of Forgiveness: Forgiving Ourselves and Others through God's Grace
by Marcia Ford 8 x 8, 176 pp, Quality PB, 978-1-59473-175-4 **$16.99**

The Sacred Art of Listening: Forty Reflections for Cultivating a Spiritual Practice
by Kay Lindahl; Illustrations by Amy Schnapper
8 x 8, 160 pp, b/w illus., Quality PB, 978-1-893361-44-7 **$16.99**

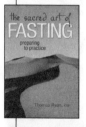

The Sacred Art of Lovingkindness: Preparing to Practice
by Rabbi Rami Shapiro; Foreword by Marcia Ford 5½ x 8½, 176 pp, Quality PB, 978-1-59473-151-8 **$16.99**

Sacred Speech: A Practical Guide for Keeping Spirit in Your Speech
by Rev. Donna Schaper 6 x 9, 176 pp, Quality PB, 978-1-59473-068-9 **$15.99**
HC, 978-1-893361-74-4 **$21.95**

Spirituality & Crafts

Contemplative Crochet: A Hands-On Guide for Interlocking Faith and Craft *by Cindy Crandall-Frazier; Foreword by Linda Skolnik*
Illuminates the spiritual lessons you can learn through crocheting.
7 x 9, 208 pp, b/w photographs, Quality PB, 978-1-59473-238-6 **$16.99**

The Knitting Way: A Guide to Spiritual Self-Discovery
by Linda Skolnik and Janice MacDaniels
Examines how you can explore and strengthen your spiritual life through knitting.
7 x 9, 240 pp, b/w photographs, Quality PB, 978-1-59473-079-5 **$16.99**

The Painting Path: Embodying Spiritual Discovery through Yoga, Brush and Color *by Linda Novick; Foreword by Richard Segalman*
Explores the divine connection you can experience through creativity.
7 x 9, 208 pp, 8-page full-color insert, plus b/w photographs
Quality PB, 978-1-59473-226-3 **$18.99**

The Quilting Path: A Guide to Spiritual Discovery through Fabric, Thread and Kabbalah *by Louise Silk*
Explores how to cultivate personal growth through quilt making.
7 x 9, 192 pp, b/w photographs and illustrations, Quality PB, 978-1-59473-206-5 **$16.99**

The Scrapbooking Journey: A Hands-On Guide to Spiritual Discovery
by Cory Richardson-Lauve; Foreword by Stacy Julian
Reveals how this craft can become a practice used to deepen and shape your life.
7 x 9, 176 pp, 8-page full-color insert, plus b/w photographs, Quality PB, 978-1-59473-216-4 **$18.99**

The Soulwork of Clay: A Hands-On Approach to Spirituality
by Marjory Zoet Bankson; Photographs by Peter Bankson
Takes you through the seven-step process of making clay into a pot, drawing parallels at each stage to the process of spiritual growth.
7 x 9, 192 pp, b/w photographs, Quality PB, 978-1-59473-249-2 **$16.99**

Kabbalah / Enneagram
(Books from Jewish Lights Publishing, SkyLight Paths' sister imprint)

God in Your Body: Kabbalah, Mindfulness and Embodied Spiritual Practice
by Jay Michaelson 6 x 9, 288 pp, Quality PB Original, 978-1-58023-304-0 **$18.99**

Cast in God's Image: Discover Your Personality Type Using the Enneagram and Kabbalah
by Rabbi Howard A. Addison 7 x 9, 176 pp, Quality PB, 978-1-58023-124-4 **$16.95**

Ehyeh: A Kabbalah for Tomorrow *by Dr. Arthur Green*
6 x 9, 224 pp, Quality PB, 978-1-58023-213-5 **$16.99**

The Enneagram and Kabbalah, 2nd Edition: Reading Your Soul
by Rabbi Howard A. Addison 6 x 9, 192 pp, Quality PB, 978-1-58023-229-6 **$16.99**

The Gift of Kabbalah: Discovering the Secrets of Heaven, Renewing Your Life on Earth
by Tamar Frankiel, PhD 6 x 9, 256 pp, Quality PB, 978-1-58023-141-1 **$16.95**
HC, 978-1-58023-108-4 **$21.95**

Kabbalah: A Brief Introduction for Christians
by Tamar Frankiel, PhD 5½ x 8½, 176 pp, Quality PB, 978-1-58023-303-3 **$16.99**

Zohar: Annotated & Explained *Translation and Annotation by Dr. Daniel C. Matt*
Foreword by Andrew Harvey 5½ x 8½, 176 pp, Quality PB, 978-1-893361-51-5 **$15.99**
(A book from Jewish Lights, SkyLight Paths' sister imprint)

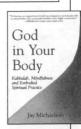

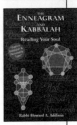

Spirituality

Next to Godliness: Finding the Sacred in Housekeeping
Edited and with Introductions by Alice Peck
Offers new perspectives on how we can reach out for the Divine.
6 x 9, 224 pp, Quality PB, 978-1-59473-214-0 **$19.99**

Bread, Body, Spirit: Finding the Sacred in Food
Edited and with Introductions by Alice Peck
Explores how food feeds our faith. 6 x 9, 224 pp, Quality PB, 978-1-59473-242-3 **$19.99**

Renewal in the Wilderness: A Spiritual Guide to Connecting with God in the Natural World *by John Lionberger*
Reveals the power of experiencing God's presence in many variations of the natural world. 6 x 9, 176 pp, b/w photos, Quality PB, 978-1-59473-219-5 **$16.99**

Honoring Motherhood: Prayers, Ceremonies and Blessings
Edited and with Introductions by Lynn L. Caruso
Journey through the seasons of motherhood. 5 x 7¼, 272 pp, HC, 978-1-59473-239-3 **$19.99**

Soul Fire: Accessing Your Creativity *by Rev. Thomas Ryan, CSP*
Learn to cultivate your creative spirit. 6 x 9, 160 pp, Quality PB, 978-1-59473-243-0 **$16.99**

Technology & Spirituality: How the Information Revolution Affects Our Spiritual Lives *by Stephen K. Spyker* 6 x 9, 176 pp, HC, 978-1-59473-218-8 **$19.99**

Money and the Way of Wisdom: Insights from the Book of Proverbs
by Timothy J. Sandoval, PhD 6 x 9, 192 pp, Quality PB, 978-1-59473-245-4 **$16.99**

Awakening the Spirit, Inspiring the Soul
30 Stories of Interspiritual Discovery in the Community of Faiths
Edited by Brother Wayne Teasdale and Martha Howard, MD; Foreword by Joan Borysenko, PhD
6 x 9, 224 pp, HC, 978-1-59473-039-9 **$21.99**

Creating a Spiritual Retirement: A Guide to the Unseen Possibilities in Our Lives
by Molly Srode 6 x 9, 208 pp, b/w photos, Quality PB, 978-1-59473-050-4 **$14.99**
HC, 978-1-893361-75-1 **$19.95**

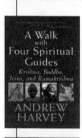

Finding Hope: Cultivating God's Gift of a Hopeful Spirit
by Marcia Ford 8 x 8, 200 pp, Quality PB, 978-1-59473-211-9 **$16.99**

The Geography of Faith: Underground Conversations on Religious, Political and Social Change *by Daniel Berrigan and Robert Coles* 6 x 9, 224 pp, Quality PB, 978-1-893361-40-9 **$16.95**

Jewish Spirituality: A Brief Introduction for Christians *by Lawrence Kushner*
5½ x 8½, 112 pp, Quality PB, 978-1-58023-150-3 **$12.95** *(A book from Jewish Lights, SkyLight Paths' sister imprint)*

Journeys of Simplicity: Traveling Light with Thomas Merton, Bashō, Edward Abbey, Annie Dillard & Others *by Philip Harnden*
5 x 7¼, 144 pp, Quality PB, 978-1-59473-181-5 **$12.99** 128 pp, HC, 978-1-893361-76-8 **$16.95**

Keeping Spiritual Balance As We Grow Older: More than 65 Creative Ways to Use Purpose, Prayer, and the Power of Spirit to Build a Meaningful Retirement
by Molly and Bernie Srode 8 x 8, 224 pp, Quality PB, 978-1-59473-042-9 **$16.99**

Spirituality 101: The Indispensable Guide to Keeping—or Finding—Your Spiritual Life on Campus *by Harriet L. Schwartz, with contributions from college students at nearly thirty campuses across the United States* 6 x 9, 272 pp, Quality PB, 978-1-59473-000-9 **$16.99**

Spiritually Incorrect: Finding God in All the Wrong Places *by Dan Wakefield; Illus. by Marian DelVecchio* 5½ x 8½, 192 pp, b/w illus., Quality PB, 978-1-59473-137-2 **$15.99**

Spiritual Manifestos: Visions for Renewed Religious Life in America from Young Spiritual Leaders of Many Faiths *Edited by Niles Elliot Goldstein; Preface by Martin E. Marty*
6 x 9, 256 pp, HC, 978-1-893361-09-6 **$21.95**

A Walk with Four Spiritual Guides: Krishna, Buddha, Jesus, and Ramakrishna
by Andrew Harvey 5½ x 8½, 192 pp, 10 b/w photos & illus., Quality PB, 978-1-59473-138-9 **$15.99**

What Matters: Spiritual Nourishment for Head and Heart
by Frederick Franck 5 x 7¼, 128 pp, 50+ b/w illus., HC, 978-1-59473-013-9 **$16.99**

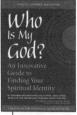

Who Is My God?, 2nd Edition: An Innovative Guide to Finding Your Spiritual Identity
Created by the Editors at SkyLight Paths 6 x 9, 160 pp, Quality PB, 978-1-59473-014-6 **$15.99**

Spirituality of the Seasons

Autumn: A Spiritual Biography of the Season
Edited by Gary Schmidt and Susan M. Felch; Illustrations by Mary Azarian
Rejoice in autumn as a time of preparation and reflection. Includes Wendell Berry, David James Duncan, Robert Frost, A. Bartlett Giamatti, E. B. White, P. D. James, Julian of Norwich, Garret Keizer, Tracy Kidder, Anne Lamott, May Sarton.
6 x 9, 320 pp, 5 b/w illus., Quality PB, 978-1-59473-118-1 **$18.99**

Spring: A Spiritual Biography of the Season
Edited by Gary Schmidt and Susan M. Felch; Illustrations by Mary Azarian
Explore the gentle unfurling of spring and reflect on how nature celebrates rebirth and renewal. Includes Jane Kenyon, Lucy Larcom, Harry Thurston, Nathaniel Hawthorne, Noel Perrin, Annie Dillard, Martha Ballard, Barbara Kingsolver, Dorothy Wordsworth, Donald Hall, David Brill, Lionel Basney, Isak Dinesen, Paul Laurence Dunbar. 6 x 9, 352 pp, 6 b/w illus., Quality PB, 978-1-59473-246-1 **$18.99**

Summer: A Spiritual Biography of the Season
Edited by Gary Schmidt and Susan M. Felch; Illustrations by Barry Moser
"A sumptuous banquet.... These selections lift up an exquisite wholeness found within an everyday sophistication."— ★ *Publishers Weekly* starred review
Includes Anne Lamott, Luci Shaw, Ray Bradbury, Richard Selzer, Thomas Lynch, Walt Whitman, Carl Sandburg, Sherman Alexie, Madeleine L'Engle, Jamaica Kincaid.
6 x 9, 304 pp, 5 b/w illus., Quality PB, 978-1-59473-183-9 **$18.99**
HC, 978-1-59473-083-2 **$21.99**

Winter: A Spiritual Biography of the Season
Edited by Gary Schmidt and Susan M. Felch; Illustrations by Barry Moser
"This outstanding anthology features top-flight nature and spirituality writers on the fierce, inexorable season of winter.... Remarkably lively and warm, despite the icy subject." — ★ *Publishers Weekly* starred review
Includes Will Campbell, Rachel Carson, Annie Dillard, Donald Hall, Ron Hansen, Jane Kenyon, Jamaica Kincaid, Barry Lopez, Kathleen Norris, John Updike, E. B. White.
6 x 9, 288 pp, 6 b/w illus., Deluxe PB w/flaps, 978-1-893361-92-8 **$18.95**

Spirituality / Animal Companions

Blessing the Animals: Prayers and Ceremonies to Celebrate God's Creatures, Wild and Tame *Edited by Lynn L. Caruso*
5¼ x 7¼, 256 pp, Quality PB, 978-1-59473-253-9 **$15.99**; HC, 978-1-59473-145-7 **$19.99**

Remembering My Pet: A Kid's Own Spiritual Workbook for When a Pet Dies
by Nechama Liss-Levinson, PhD, and Rev. Molly Phinney Baskette, MDiv; Foreword by Lynn L. Caruso
8 x 10, 48 pp, 2-color text, HC, 978-1-59473-221-3 **$16.99**

What Animals Can Teach Us about Spirituality: Inspiring Lessons from Wild and Tame Creatures *by Diana L. Guerrero* 6 x 9, 176 pp, Quality PB, 978-1-893361-84-3 **$16.95**

Spirituality—A Week Inside

Come and Sit: A Week Inside Meditation Centers
by Marcia Z. Nelson; Foreword by Wayne Teasdale
6 x 9, 224 pp, b/w photos, Quality PB, 978-1-893361-35-5 **$16.95**

Lighting the Lamp of Wisdom: A Week Inside a Yoga Ashram
by John Ittner; Foreword by Dr. David Frawley
6 x 9, 192 pp, 10+ b/w photos, Quality PB, 978-1-893361-52-2 **$15.95**

Making a Heart for God: A Week Inside a Catholic Monastery
by Dianne Aprile; Foreword by Brother Patrick Hart, ocso
6 x 9, 224 pp, b/w photos, Quality PB, 978-1-893361-49-2 **$16.95**

Waking Up: A Week Inside a Zen Monastery
by Jack Maguire; Foreword by John Daido Loori, Roshi
6 x 9, 224 pp, b/w photos, Quality PB, 978-1-893361-55-3 **$16.95**; HC, 978-1-893361-13-3 **$21.95**

Prayer / Meditation

Sacred Attention: A Spiritual Practice for Finding God in the Moment
by Margaret D. McGee
Framed on the Christian liturgical year, this inspiring guide explores ways to develop a practice of attention as a means of talking—and listening—to God.
6 x 9, 144 pp, HC, 978-1-59473-232-4 **$19.99**

Women Pray: Voices through the Ages, from Many Faiths, Cultures and Traditions
Edited and with Introductions by Monica Furlong
5 x 7¼, 256 pp, Quality PB, 978-1-59473-071-9 **$15.99**

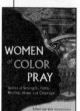

Women of Color Pray: Voices of Strength, Faith, Healing, Hope and Courage   *Edited and with Introductions by Christal M. Jackson*
Through these prayers, poetry, lyrics, meditations and affirmations, you will share in the strong and undeniable connection women of color share with God.
5 x 7¼, 208 pp, Quality PB, 978-1-59473-077-1 **$15.99**

Secrets of Prayer: A Multifaith Guide to Creating Personal Prayer in Your Life   *by Nancy Corcoran, CSJ*
This compelling, multifaith guidebook offers you companionship and encouragement on the journey to a healthy prayer life. 6 x 9, 160 pp, Quality PB, 978-1-59473-215-7 **$16.99**

Prayers to an Evolutionary God
by William Cleary; Afterword by Diarmuid O'Murchu
Inspired by the spiritual and scientific teachings of Diarmuid O'Murchu and Teilhard de Chardin, reveals that religion and science can be combined to create an expanding view of the universe—an evolutionary faith.
6 x 9, 208 pp, HC, 978-1-59473-006-1 **$21.99**

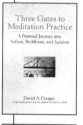

The Art of Public Prayer: Not for Clergy Only   *by Lawrence A. Hoffman*
6 x 9, 288 pp, Quality PB, 978-1-893361-06-5 **$18.99**

A Heart of Stillness: A Complete Guide to Learning the Art of Meditation
by David A. Cooper 5½ x 8½, 272 pp, Quality PB, 978-1-893361-03-4 **$16.95**

Meditation without Gurus: A Guide to the Heart of Practice
by Clark Strand 5½ x 8½, 192 pp, Quality PB, 978-1-893361-93-5 **$16.95**

Praying with Our Hands: 21 Practices of Embodied Prayer from the World's Spiritual Traditions   *by Jon M. Sweeney; Photographs by Jennifer J. Wilson; Foreword by Mother Tessa Bielecki; Afterword by Taitetsu Unno, PhD*
8 x 8, 96 pp, 22 duotone photos, Quality PB, 978-1-893361-16-4 **$16.95**

Silence, Simplicity & Solitude: A Complete Guide to Spiritual Retreat at Home
by David A. Cooper 5½ x 8½, 336 pp, Quality PB, 978-1-893361-04-1 **$16.95**

Three Gates to Meditation Practice: A Personal Journey into Sufism, Buddhism, and Judaism   *by David A. Cooper* 5½ x 8½, 240 pp, Quality PB, 978-1-893361-22-5 **$16.95**

Prayer / M. Basil Pennington, OCSO

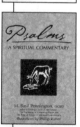

Finding Grace at the Center, 3rd Ed.: The Beginning of Centering Prayer   *with Thomas Keating, OCSO, and Thomas E. Clarke, SJ; Foreword by Rev. Cynthia Bourgeault, PhD*
A practical guide to a simple and beautiful form of meditative prayer.
5 x 7¼, 128 pp, Quality PB, 978-1-59473-182-2 **$12.99**

The Monks of Mount Athos: A Western Monk's Extraordinary Spiritual Journey on Eastern Holy Ground   *Foreword by Archimandrite Dionysios*
Explores the landscape, the monastic communities, and the food of Athos.
6 x 9, 256 pp, 10+ b/w drawings, Quality PB, 978-1-893361-78-2 **$18.95**

Psalms: A Spiritual Commentary   *Illustrations by Phillip Ratner*
Reflections on some of the most beloved passages from the Bible's most widely read book. 6 x 9, 176 pp, 24 full-page b/w illus., Quality PB, 978-1-59473-234-8 **$16.99**
HC, 978-1-59473-141-9 **$19.99**

The Song of Songs: A Spiritual Commentary   *Illustrations by Phillip Ratner*
Explore the Bible's most challenging mystical text.
6 x 9, 160 pp, 14 b/w illus., Quality PB, 978-1-59473-235-3 **$16.99**; HC, 978-1-59473-004-7 **$19.99**

Sacred Texts—SkyLight Illuminations Series

Offers today's spiritual seeker an accessible entry into the great classic texts of the world's spiritual traditions. Each classic is presented in an accessible translation, with facing pages of guided commentary from experts, giving you the keys you need to understand the history, context and meaning of the text. This series enables you, whatever your background, to experience and understand classic spiritual texts directly, and to make them a part of your life.

CHRISTIANITY

The End of Days: Essential Selections from Apocalyptic Texts—
Annotated & Explained *Annotation by Robert G. Clouse*
Helps you understand the complex Christian visions of the end of the world.
5½ x 8½, 224 pp, Quality PB, 978-1-59473-170-9 **$16.99**

The Hidden Gospel of Matthew: Annotated & Explained
Translation & Annotation by Ron Miller
Takes you deep into the text cherished around the world to discover the words and events that have the strongest connection to the historical Jesus.
5½ x 8½, 272 pp, Quality PB, 978-1-59473-038-2 **$16.99**

The Lost Sayings of Jesus: Teachings from Ancient Christian, Jewish, Gnostic and Islamic Sources—Annotated & Explained
Translation & Annotation by Andrew Phillip Smith; Foreword by Stephan A. Hoeller
This collection of more than three hundred sayings depicts Jesus as a Wisdom teacher who speaks to people of all faiths as a mystic and spiritual master.
5½ x 8½, 240 pp, Quality PB, 978-1-59473-172-3 **$16.99**

Philokalia: The Eastern Christian Spiritual Texts—Selections Annotated & Explained *Annotation by Allyne Smith; Translation by G. E. H. Palmer, Phillip Sherrard and Bishop Kallistos Ware*
The first approachable introduction to the wisdom of the Philokalia, which is the classic text of Eastern Christian spirituality.
5½ x 8½, 240 pp, Quality PB, 978-1-59473-103-7 **$16.99**

The Sacred Writings of Paul: Selections Annotated & Explained
Translation & Annotation by Ron Miller
Explores the apostle Paul's core message of spiritual equality, freedom and joy.
5½ x 8½, 224 pp, Quality PB, 978-1-59473-213-3 **$16.99**

Sex Texts from the Bible: Selections Annotated & Explained
Translation & Annotation by Teresa J. Hornsby; Foreword by Amy-Jill Levine
Offers surprising insight into our modern sexual lives.
5½ x 8½, 208 pp, Quality PB, 978-1-59473-217-1 **$16.99**

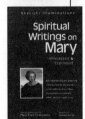

Spiritual Writings on Mary: Annotated & Explained
Annotation by Mary Ford-Grabowsky; Foreword by Andrew Harvey
Examines the role of Mary, the mother of Jesus, as a source of inspiration in history and in life today. 5½ x 8½, 288 pp, Quality PB, 978-1-59473-001-6 **$16.99**

The Way of a Pilgrim: The Jesus Prayer Journey—Annotated & Explained
Translation & Annotation by Gleb Pokrovsky; Foreword by Andrew Harvey
This classic of Russian spirituality is the delightful account of one man who sets out to learn the prayer of the heart, also known as the "Jesus prayer."
5½ x 8½, 160 pp, Illus., Quality PB, 978-1-893361-31-7 **$14.95**

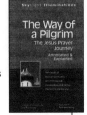

Sacred Texts—cont.

MORMONISM

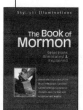

The Book of Mormon: Selections Annotated & Explained
Annotation by Jana Riess; Foreword by Phyllis Tickle
Explores the sacred epic that is cherished by more than twelve million members of the LDS church as the keystone of their faith.
5½ x 8½ , 272 pp, Quality PB, 978-1-59473-076-4 **$16.99**

NATIVE AMERICAN

Native American Stories of the Sacred: Annotated & Explained
Retold & Annotated by Evan T. Pritchard
Intended for more than entertainment, these teaching tales contain elegantly simple illustrations of time-honored truths.
5½ x 8½, 272 pp, Quality PB, 978-1-59473-112-9 **$16.99**

GNOSTICISM

Gnostic Writings on the Soul: Annotated & Explained
Translation & Annotation by Andrew Phillip Smith; Foreword by Stephan A. Hoeller
Reveals the inspiring ways your soul can remember and return to its unique, divine purpose.
5½ x 8½, 144 pp, Quality PB, 978-1-59473-220-1 **$16.99**

The Gospel of Philip: Annotated & Explained
Translation & Annotation by Andrew Phillip Smith; Foreword by Stevan Davies
Reveals otherwise unrecorded sayings of Jesus and fragments of Gnostic mythology.
5½ x 8½, 160 pp, Quality PB, 978-1-59473-111-2 **$16.99**

The Gospel of Thomas: Annotated & Explained
Translation & Annotation by Stevan Davies Sheds new light on the origins of Christianity and portrays Jesus as a wisdom-loving sage.
5½ x 8½, 192 pp, Quality PB, 978-1-893361-45-4 **$16.99**

The Secret Book of John: The Gnostic Gospel—Annotated & Explained
Translation & Annotation by Stevan Davies The most significant and influential text of the ancient Gnostic religion.
5½ x 8½, 208 pp, Quality PB, 978-1-59473-082-5 **$16.99**

JUDAISM

The Divine Feminine in Biblical Wisdom Literature
Selections Annotated & Explained
Translation & Annotation by Rabbi Rami Shapiro; Foreword by Rev. Cynthia Bourgeault, PhD
Uses the Hebrew books of Psalms, Proverbs, Song of Songs, Ecclesiastes and Job, Wisdom literature and the Wisdom of Solomon to clarify who Wisdom is.
5½ x 8½, 240 pp, Quality PB, 978-1-59473-109-9 **$16.99**

Ethics of the Sages: Pirke Avot—Annotated & Explained
Translation & Annotation by Rabbi Rami Shapiro Clarifies the ethical teachings of the early Rabbis. 5½ x 8½, 192 pp, Quality PB, 978-1-59473-207-2 **$16.99**

Hasidic Tales: Annotated & Explained
Translation & Annotation by Rabbi Rami Shapiro
Introduces the legendary tales of the impassioned Hasidic rabbis, presenting them as stories rather than as parables. 5½ x 8½, 240 pp, Quality PB, 978-1-893361-86-7 **$16.95**

The Hebrew Prophets: Selections Annotated & Explained
Translation & Annotation by Rabbi Rami Shapiro; Foreword by Zalman M. Schachter-Shalomi
Focuses on the central themes covered by all the Hebrew prophets.
5½ x 8½, 224 pp, Quality PB, 978-1-59473-037-5 **$16.99**

Zohar: Annotated & Explained *Translation & Annotation by Daniel C. Matt*
The best-selling author of *The Essential Kabbalah* brings together in one place the most important teachings of the Zohar, the canonical text of Jewish mystical tradition.
5½ x 8½, 176 pp, Quality PB, 978-1-893361-51-5 **$15.99**